The Complete Business Writing Kit

The Complete Business Writing Kit

All the Skills You Need in 10 Self-Instructional Lessons

Olivia Stockard
with Fredric Margolis

WILEY

JOHN WILEY & SONS
New York • Chichester • Brisbane • Toronto • Singapore

This publication is designed to provide accurate and
authoritative information in regard to the subject
matter covered. It is sold with the understanding that
the publisher is not engaged in rendering legal, accounting,
or other professional service. If legal advice or other
expert assistance is required, the services of a competent
professional person should be sought. *From a Declaration
of Principles jointly adopted by a Committee of the
American Bar Association and a Committee of Publishers.*

Library of Congress Cataloging in Publication Data

Stockard, Olivia.
    The complete business writing kit : all the skills you need in 10
self-instructional lessons / Olivia Stockard with Fredric Margolis.
      p.   cm.

    Bibliography: p.
    1. Business writing. I. Margolis, Fredric. II. Title.

HF5718.3.S76 1988
808'.066651—dc19   88-15518
                                                CIP

ISBN 0-471-61282-0

Printed in the United States of America

10 9 8 7 6 5 4 3

For Steve

Preface

I have written this book for the person who has already acquired a sense of good writing and now needs to develop it for business writing.

You probably first became acquainted with good writing in high school or college. You have read a number of novels, essays, and, if your major was a technical subject, tracts and texts of a technical nature. You may enjoy reading poetry. Undoubtedly, you read newspapers and magazines frequently.

My point is, you read a lot. Therefore, you have gained a concept of good writing, whether you're especially conscious of it or not.

You also know how to write sentences and paragraphs. The terms used in grammatical analysis may elude you, but you know a sentence from a nonsentence and writing that makes sense as opposed to nonsense. You have also probably had to write your share of term papers, research reports, and perhaps even a thesis.

Why, then, do you need this book at all? Because at first glance, business reports and memorandums may seem very different from the kinds of papers you have been asked to write before. One purpose of this book is to strip away some of the mystique that has come to surround these forms in recent years. For example, what is that strange beast, the memorandum, that business people sometimes speak of with such trepidation? Just a short report. What is that even more awesome animal, the "executive memorandum"? A memorandum written from one executive to another. What is a memo? The abbreviation for memorandum.

Unlike many books about business writing, therefore, this one will *not* tell you that you have to unlearn everything you learned in academic writing classes to be a good business writer. Those classes gave you the right foundation. You will learn how to apply many of the principles and techniques you already know to business writing.

Somewhere in your travels, however, you may have gained a concept of writing style that will not communicate effectively to a business reader. Your writing instructors, for example, were *paid* to read your writing. The time and trouble they took to involve themselves in your prose would not be found in people you work with. Writers of previous centuries wrote for readers who had leisure and patience. The exact opposite would be said of most business people today.

Your worst stylistic models are likely to be some of the routine reports and correspondence that cross your desk every day. The same bad habits get passed down from generation to generation, especially in large corporations. You'll need to develop some standards of taste before you can decide what's worth imitating in your colleagues' writing and what isn't.

The examples presented in this book are drawn primarily from reports written in large corporations and small businesses. You will be given the opportunity to confront some of this actual business writing, react to it, and edit it. You will also produce some writing of your own. Using my discussions of other people's work, you will be asked to make judgments and set your own standards. This is ultimately what every writer must do for himself or herself.

I encourage you to use this book to form your own concept of style—one that makes sense to you, given your audience and the situations you'll be writing about.

Acknowledgments

This book comes directly from the interior of American business. It began as an internal training text written for the Professional Development Program of Chase Manhattan Bank. Writing a self-instructional book on a subject as complex as business writing is, by any standard, a risky and adventurous undertaking. I am grateful to my former colleagues and students at Chase for taking this initial risk with me and for allowing the fruits of that labor to be shared with others.

Specific people I'd like to thank for reviewing the manuscript are John Kirk and Charles "Pete" Bailey of Chase, Gene Zelazny of McKinsey & Company, Inc., and Professor Geraldine Henze of the Graduate School of Business at Columbia University. I'd also like to thank Jim Ehret of Chase for helping me enter the world of word processing and computers when the time came to revise the manuscript.

A special thank you goes to Fred Margolis, who worked closely with me to develop the self-instructional format and exercises in this book. When I first began the project, I had my doubts that it could be done. Fred inspired and encouraged me throughout the design and writing process. He is a mentor in the truest sense of that word.

Finally, I'd like to thank my husband, Steve Elmer, for his patience, understanding, and unfailing support in this and all my endeavors.

Contents

Contents

1

Principles of Readability

Introduction to the Principles of Readability

This book is not going to tell you "how to write." It is not intended to box you in and inhibit your natural expressiveness.

It will help you write appropriately for your reader and for the occasion. It will help you become more conscious of styles of writing that may have influenced you and whether they should continue to influence you. It will encourage you to express your natural creativity and flair, even when writing for business purposes.

Before we go further, let's look at two issues. First, "Myths of Business Writing":

- You must always write in short sentences.
- You should confine yourself to one- or two-syllable words.
- Eloquence and elegance are unnecessary in business writing.
- Reports and memorandums are necessarily going to be duller than essays or literature.

The classification of these items as myths may surprise you. You may have heard that business writing necessarily lacks individuality and expressiveness. You are limited to short sentences and simple vocabulary—in line with the "KISS" rule: "Keep it simple, stupid!" Then there's that famous formula of management communication intoned by some trainers and managers: "Tell 'em what you're gonna tell 'em. Tell 'em. Tell 'em you told 'em." That's a sure-fire prescription for dullness.

Now let's consider some principles of written expression that are worth having.

- *Write in your own voice*, not an "official" voice or jargon.

- *Strive for a fresh expression*. Avoid clichés and long-winded phrases or figures of speech that you frequently see in other people's writing.
- *Don't make your reader's life unnecessarily hard*. Don't use uncommon words if common words will do just as well.
- *Get to the point*. Use active voice more often than passive. If it's possible to cut down on the number of words, do so.
- Be concerned, first and foremost, with *communicating*.

It's easy to build these two lists. It's much more difficult to understand their implications for you as a writer and their effect on your reader.

We'll begin to examine these issues by considering the impact of writing. You're going to have the opportunity to read some writing that is provocative, some that is factual, and some that is logical. As you read these three samples, don't discount any particular style merely because it doesn't appeal to you. Remember, each of these styles was purposely created to communicate in a certain way with a particular audience. Each was successful.

Example 1

In that mysterious dimension where the body meets the soul the stereotype is born and has her being. She is more body than soul, more soul than mind. To her belongs all that is beautiful, even the very word beauty itself. All that exists, exists to beautify her. . . .

The men of our civilization have stripped themselves of the fineries of the earth so that they might work more freely to plunder the universe for treasures to deck my lady in. New raw materials, new processes, new machines are all brought into her service. My lady must therefore be the chief spender as well as the chief symbol of spending ability and monetary success. While her mate toils in his factory, she totters about the smartest streets and plushiest hotels with his fortune upon her back and bosom, fingers and wrists, continuing that essential expenditure in his house which is her frame and her setting, enjoying that silken idleness which is the necessary condition of maintaining her mate's prestige and her qualification to demonstrate it. Once upon a time only the aristocratic lady could lay claim to the title of crown of creation: only her hands were white enough, her feet tiny enough, her waist narrow enough, her hair long and golden enough; but every well-to-do burgher's wife set herself up to ape my lady and to follow fashion, until my lady was forced to set herself out like a gilded doll overlaid with monstrous rubies and pearls like pigeons' eggs. Nowadays the Queen of England still considers it part of her royal female role to sport as much of the family jewelry as she can manage at any one time on all public occasions, although the male monarchs have escaped such showcase duty, which devolves exclusively upon their wives.[1]

. . . .

The writer is Germaine Greer in her highly controversial book, *The Female Eunuch*. In this paragraph from a chapter called "Stereotype," she sees her audience as people who need a good kick in the pants about the stereotype of the successful woman that many have unconsciously assimilated. In this paragraph, she challenges her readers to think about things they have probably taken for granted and never questioned.

Greer's major devices for prodding us to see this stereotype more clearly are wit and sarcasm. She points out that there is a ridiculous side to women bedecked in jewels and finery that

[1]Germaine Greer, *The Female Eunuch* (New York: McGraw-Hill, 1970), pp. 51–52. Reprinted with permission.

bespeak their husband's or some other man's status and suc-cess. Her language and its connotations are the key to her opinion: "she *totters* about the smartest streets," "*silken idle-ness*," "*ape* my lady," "*gilded* doll *overlaid* with *monstrous* ru-bies and pearls like *pigeons' eggs*." The picture painted of women who aspire to such idle symbolic status and the men who indulge them is hardly flattering. Man "*toils* in his factory . . . *stripped* . . . of the fineries of the earth" while my lady is the "chief spender" and major consumer force of the economy.

Greer not only ridicules this stereotype—she analyzes its roots. She points out that the idea basically derives from a fundamental economic and social caste system. This system, in turn, derives from work and economic independence, or the lack thereof. The burgher's wife, as her husband pursued his career, had nothing better to do than aspire to "ape" a lady of the higher classes or royalty. Meaningful work was the prov-ince of men, who found their vanity flattered by having a walk-ing status symbol around. Ultimately, the root of the stereotype lies in shallow and ignoble human values: status-seeking, envy, greed, vanity, and lack of purposeful activity in life.

Germaine Greer has undoubtedly succeeded in her goal to become a primary spokesperson for the feminist movement. She has frequently appeared on talk shows and has written many books and articles on the subject. Her voice is always forceful, irreverent, and provocative.

....

Example 2

IT PAYS TO BE ACTIVE. The new law won't allow you to write off losses up to $25,000 from rental properties unless you ac-tively participate in their operation. This "active participation test" is less stringent than the "material participation test" that applies to other passive activities. . . .

The bottom line: As long as you make significant and bona fide management decisions, you meet the test. Using a rental agent will not, by itself, leave you out in the cold.

The management decisions that count, as far as Uncle Sam is concerned, include approving tenants, deciding on rental terms, and approving capital or repair expenditures.

One last wrinkle: You won't meet this requirement if your real estate is owned through a limited partnership or for any amount of time that you hold less than a 10-percent ownership interest.

What happens if you don't actively participate—or if you own less than a 10-percent interest? Your rental loss is considered "passive," and you may not deduct it from your regular income. You may deduct it only from income generated by other passive investments.[2]

....

This is an excerpt from one of the clearest and most readable books probably ever written on taxes. It is called *The Price Waterhouse Guide to the New Tax Law*. The book was ghost-written by Donna Carpenter, a professional writer, working with a team of Price Waterhouse tax specialists. Since the audience is anyone trying to understand the new tax law, the book is written in a way that will not be off-putting to nontechnical readers and that will motivate them to stay with the book.

For example, throughout the book (which is 251 pages), the writer uses simple, nontechnical terms whenever possible. Often, as in this excerpt, she explains a technical concept like "active participation" by speaking about it in colloquial language: "meet the test," "out in the cold," "last wrinkle," "Uncle Sam," and "bottom line." These expressions, which might sound clichéd in another context, are refreshing here.

---

[2]*The Price Waterhouse Guide to the New Tax Law*, Intro. by Roscoe L. Egger, Jr. (New York: Bantam Books, 1986), pp. 42–43.

Other devices she uses to keep the reader reading are short, pithy paragraphs. The book as a whole is divided into many small chunks of subject matter. Many of them have witty or catchy subtitles: "It Pays to Be Active," "Risky Business," "Neither a Borrower Nor a Lender Be." It helps to enjoy a chuckle if you have to read about taxes.

That a subject as technical as tax laws can be made understandable to the general public should be a lesson to anyone who thinks he cannot explain his technical world to laymen.

Example 3

I deny not, but that it is of greatest concernment in the Church and Commonwealth, to have a vigilant eye how books demean themselves, as well as men; and thereafter to confine, imprison, and do sharpest justice on them as malefactors. For books are not absolutely dead things, but do contain a potency of life in them to be as active as that soul was whose progeny they are; nay, they do preserve as in a vial the purest efficacy and extraction of that living intellect that bred them. I know they are as lively, and as vigorously productive, as those fabulous dragon's teeth; and being sown up and down, may chance to spring up armed men. And yet, on the other hand, unless wariness be used, as good almost kill a man as kill a good book; who kills a man kills a reasonable creature, God's image; but he who destroys a good book, kills reason itself, kills the image of God, as it were in the eye.[3]

This example is from a pamphlet entitled "Areopagitica," published in 1644 by the poet John Milton. It was written in re-

[3]John Milton, "Areopagitica," excerpted and reprinted in *The College Survey of English Literature*, Ed. Alexander M. Witherspoon, Shorter Edition, Revised (New York: Harcourt, Brace and World, 1951), p. 427.

sponse to an act of Parliament requiring that all books and pamphlets be licensed by an official censor before publication. Milton saw this act as having disastrous consequences for freedom of the press. He also had a personal interest in that his divorce pamphlets were being published without official license and were scandalizing people both in and out of Parliament.[4]

Milton's audience, basically the English aristocracy, were highly educated in the classics and the Bible. Thus the "dragon's teeth" analogy, an allusion to a story in Ovid's *Metamorphoses,* would have been familiar to them. In fact, readers expected writers to "embellish" their writing with such allusions to enrich the context and stimulate the reader's thinking.

The Bible was thought in Milton's time to be the repository of all moral wisdom. Thus elaborating on the logic of a Biblical point would give that point great moral validity and gravity for the reader. Milton explores this logic:

....

(x) The Bible teaches that man is reasonable because he is made in the image of God.

(y) Killing a man is like killing God.

Therefore, killing a book, the product of man's reason, is like killing Reason itself, and therefore God, the prototype and source of Reason.

....

Circuitous reasoning, you say? Not to Milton's readers, who would not have thought of this merely in syllogistic terms. *Reason,* to Milton's readers, meant the highest part of man, his

------

[4]*The College Survey of English Literature,* p. 426.

mind or spirit. It was this aspect of man that made him higher than animals but a little lower than the angels. To "kill a book," the repository of reason or man's "divine part," would be a heinous act indeed.

A common belief system and body of learning characterized Milton's audience. They expected him to argue from a tradition they understood and revered. In short, an argument needed a moral basis to be persuasive. In addition, readers expected writers to demonstrate their learning and challenge the reader's intellect. It was not easy to win someone over to another point of view.

All these writers show a sensitivity to and understanding of their audience's needs, biases, and expectations. Germaine Greer knew that people have to be shaken up, perhaps even angered at times, to reconsider old stereotypes. The tax writer knew that tax is a boring and virtually incomprehensible subject to most people. Thus she was concerned to simplify, enliven, and speak almost colloquially to help readers stay motivated to learn about the subject. Milton was concerned not to change his audience's beliefs but rather to deepen their understanding of what those beliefs were based on. Thus they would more likely be convinced by his arguments.

These writers also illustrate how styles have changed as audiences have changed. Milton's readers had the leisure, learning, and patience to follow his subtle arguments. His sentences were clearly not written for people in a hurry to "get on with business." Germaine Greer, like Milton, is a polemist, but how her style differs from his. Her sentences are just as long but have a hard-hitting rhythm; their impact is emotional rather than reflective or logical. The tax writer's sentences are much shorter, her vocabulary simpler, and the writing less "literary" than Milton's or Greer's. The subject is not emotional, nor is it one that readers care to ponder any more than they have to. She was clearly aware of this.

You might say at this point, "This is all very interesting but it has nothing to do with me. I just write business letters and memorandums. I'm not a literary type."

You're right and you're wrong. You're right in that, unlike polemists such as Greer and Milton or even expository writers such as the tax writer, you write to a particular person or small group, not to a general audience. Your tone in a business letter or report would certainly never be sarcastic like Greer's. If someone doesn't like her style he won't buy her book—nothing much worse can happen to her. But you could lose a valuable customer or even your job.

On the other hand, anyone who has read a good deal in his life is a "literary type" whether he knows it or not. The rhythms of sentences you've read are implanted in your ear. Anyone who says, "That sentence sounds abrupt—it needs a few words to round it out," has read Milton or some other seventeenth-, eighteenth-, or nineteenth-century prose stylist at some point in his life. And he retained the rhythm of those sentences in his subconscious.

To write at your best either for business or for some other forum, you must become conscious of what models you've assimilated and why you gravitate toward a certain style in writing. You also need to think more consciously about your readers and what will be most effective with them in various situations.

In short, all public writing—even poems and novels—is someone's attempt to *communicate* something to someone else. This means that your style need not be a hard, fossilized voice that imitates any one writing style, but rather a flexible medium that speaks in tones appropriate to the situation and the reader. Simply stated, you must vary your writing style to suit each situation and reader you face.* Sometimes you'll want to state facts clearly, sometimes you'll want to present a logical argument, sometimes you'll want to be provocative or persuasive. Your intent and therefore, your style, will not always be the same.

To become accomplished in this way of writing means acquiring technique and not merely going on "feel," imitation of other people's writing, or subconscious promptings. It means becoming conscious of the principles of readability.

Becoming Conscious of the Principles of Readability

Let's talk now about what generally appeals to you as a business reader and writer.

Since you've done a lot of reading, you have already discovered that some pieces of writing are easier to read than others. For example, you may have found Milton's prose slow-going because the vocabulary and allusions were unfamiliar and the sentences were long.

Milton's audience, however, would have found his style readable. His prose is difficult for readers today because beliefs have changed and tastes in writing have changed. Newspapers and magazines have had a major impact on people's concept of style. The essence of journalism is "concise and to the point." This is what many people today think of as readable writing.

---

*John S. Fielden has written an excellent article on this subject entitled "What Do You Mean, You Don't Like My Style?" in the *Harvard Business Review,* May–June 1982, pp. 128–138.

Along with journalism, another major stylistic influence on most business people is what I call an "internally approved" style used in their profession or organization. In fact, many large organizations develop an internal style that employees perceive as the "right way to write." Unfortunately, the more any style is copied, the more it becomes clichéd and lifeless. Since it is more of an expedient than a true choice, it spreads, for the most part, by unthinking imitation.

This kind of writing has been given many names: gobbledygook, officialese, bureaucratese, and The Official Style.[5] Although most people would agree that this kind of writing is not easy to read, everybody who works in an organization will be accustomed to that company's particular Official Style and will be likely to use it.

Here's an example of some gross officialese. Yet some people—those trained by the organizational environment to decipher the style—would to some degree find it readable.

....

The rate of postage for zone-rated mail which is mailed at or addressed to an armed forces post office and which is transported directly to or from such an office at the expense of the Department of Defense, without transiting the forty-eight contiguous states, shall be the applicable local zone rate; provided, however, that if the distance from the point of debarkation to the place of delivery is greater than the local zone for such mail, postage shall be assessed on the basis of the distance from the place of mailing to the embarkation point or the distance from the point of debarkation to the place of delivery of such mail, as the case may be.

....

---

[5]Richard A. Lanham, *Revising Prose* (New York: Charles Scribner's Sons, 1979), p. 25.

This example probably turned you off. Even the Army was turned off enough to show it as an example of bad writing.[6] Like many other organizations, the Army has tried to raise its standard of writing. Once bad stylistic habits are ingrained, however, efforts to change or improve them can become a major problem, requiring enormous training and relearning by employees.

You might reasonably ask at this point, "Why should I or my organization bother thinking about prose style as long as we can decipher one another's messages? Why shouldn't I write the way everybody else in the company does? Give it to them the way they want it!"

I ask you to read and reflect for a moment on this passage by another writer observing the proliferation of officialese today.

....

The Official Style runs from school days to retirement. As soon as you realize that you live "in a system," whether P.S. 41, the University of California, or the Department of Agriculture, you start developing The Official Style. Used unthinkingly, it provides the quickest tip-off that you have become system-sick, and look at life only through the system's eyes. It is a scribal style, ritualized, formulaic, using a private vocabulary to describe a particular kind of world. And it is, increasingly, the only kind of prose style America ever sees.[7]

....

When you give up your own voice to an official voice, to some degree you give up your own ideas and ability to think independently. This violates perhaps the most fundamental princi-

---

[6]The excerpt is taken from a training pamphlet entitled "How to Write Right for Us!" United States Army Training and Doctrine Command (Fort Monroe, Virginia, August 1980), pp. 2–3.
[7]Lanham, *Revising Prose*, p. 25.

ple of good writing. With that goes your creativity and ability to *have* new ideas. In fact, you may be giving up your ability to make a real contribution to your organization and to experience personal growth in your career. New ideas, problem-solving ability, and genuine innovation are the lifeblood of business.

If you adopt a company's officialese, you may also find yourself trapped by this style and unable to express yourself clearly. This can be a problem when you are writing for the general public or if you change jobs or perhaps even divisions within a company.

In short, you should work to develop *your own style* based on the principles of readability. This is not easy. You have to be knowledgeable about these principles before you can use them. You'll also need the technique to modify and adapt your style to different readers and situations.

By way of analogy, think of modern painters and their work. They do not merely splash paint on canvas, though it may sometimes appear that way. They have studied the traditions and evolution of style in painting. If they violate a tradition—say, the realistic tradition—they have chosen to do so for a specific reason. They are competent in using traditional styles and techniques. Pablo Picasso, for example, was an extremely accomplished realistic painter and draftsman by the time he was twenty. When he painted eyes in the middle of foreheads, he had *chosen* to do so.

One of the best ways to learn about what makes writing readable is to recognize what is making someone else's writing easy or difficult to read. It's initially easier to be more objective about someone else's work than your own because you are the reader undergoing either a pleasurable or a painful experience.

Let's go back to the painting analogy in a slightly different way. People who are inexperienced in looking at paintings still know what they like. People who are experienced observers of art know what they like and why they like it, and are more likely to recognize pieces that they will truly like for a longer period of time.

Now you're going to have the opportunity to read and react to some examples of business writing. They are not all drawn from the same kinds of documents so their purposes are different. You will be asked only to react to the way they are written.

Exercise: Reacting to Other People's Writing

To improve the readability of your own writing, you will first need to recognize what you like and why you like it. As a first step, read the following four paragraphs. First, circle *one* of the five descriptions that best describes your reaction to the paragraph. Then describe your reaction in a phrase of your own in the space provided.

....

Example 1

While it is expected that all known and foreseeable significant credit issues will be fully dealt with and resolved in the business and strategic planning processes, it will not always be possible to adequately anticipate market opportunities and/or conditions that may occur before the next scheduled review. A business unit may want to alter its plans and establish new programs for existing or prospective markets. A change in direction that has not been included in the business and/or strategic planning process and which has significant potential for altering risk in the units' portfolio must be referred to the next higher management level for approval where the significance is weighed in terms of all the business units reporting thereto. If in that context the matter is considered significant, it is to be escalated up in accordance with the business and strategic planning processes.

(A) Clear—easy to read
(B) Clear—required some reasonable effort
(C) Clear—required substantial effort and rereading
(D) Partially clear—required substantial rereading
(E) Unclear—tended to give up

Describe your reaction: _____

_____

_____

_____

_____

....

Example 2

Jargon is the language of specialists and is appropriate when writing or speaking to other specialists in the same field. People conversant in a jargon usually aren't offended by it. But a writer should never assume a reader's familiarity with jargon. Don't make the mistake of assuming that "anyone who knows anything about business will know what I mean when I write of cash cows." Don't bet on it. Jargon tends to be more local than you think, and many successful executives have never heard of cash cows and would prefer not to.

(A) Clear—easy to read
(B) Clear—required some reasonable effort
(C) Clear—required substantial effort and rereading
(D) Partially clear—required substantial rereading
(E) Unclear—tended to give up

Describe your reaction: _____

_____

_____

_____

_____

....

Example 3

Cyclical sales growth is partially controlled by continuous expansion and sufficient capitalization. Forecasting tools enable the company to plan ahead in order to control costs and protect profit margins. Quality store management and incentive programs also offset downturns to sales and/or margins. Since the company lacks diversification, cyclicality must be partially mitigated by management.

(A) Clear—easy to read
(B) Clear—required some reasonable effort
(C) Clear—required substantial effort and rereading
(D) Partially clear—required substantial rereading
(E) Unclear—tended to give up

Describe your reaction: _____

_____

_____

_____

_____

....

Example 4

As part of the ongoing effort to more fully utilize the program's Spread and Projection System for production work, the Systems Committee has decided it is necessary to establish appropriate contacts with line areas and other interested parties to determine the acceptability of currently produced computerized spread reports for inclusion in production account files. It is also felt that an "internal" review of these documents would be valuable prior to the soliciting of "external" comments.

(A) Clear—easy to read
(B) Clear—required some reasonable effort
(C) Clear—required substantial effort and rereading
(D) Partially clear—required substantial rereading
(E) Unclear—tended to give up

Describe your reaction: _____
_____
_____
_____
_____

....

Commentary: Reacting to Other People's Writing

Example 1

You probably responded with (D) or (E) for the first example. Other readers have written descriptions such as:

- complex
- not direct
- convoluted sentences
- vague vocabulary
- sounds as if a lawyer wrote it

To a great degree, all these descriptions are obvious. Even though this writing is not easy to get through, it happens much too often in business writing.

Some of the reasons this kind of writing happens frequently are:

- People feel their writing must sound impressive.
- People feel they must explain every aspect of a situation, resulting in repetitiveness.
- People write as they think instead of organizing a plan for their thoughts before they write.
- People have adopted a bureaucratic style common to the company.

Example 2

Let's look at the second paragraph. This example is from a handbook on business writing entitled *From Murk to Masterpiece: Style for Business Writing*, by Geraldine Henze (Homewood, Ill.: Richard D. Irwin, Inc., 1984), p. 43.

You probably scored that (A) or (B). This too is somewhat obvious. Some of the phrases other readers have used to describe it are:

- clear
- direct
- conversational
- writing has punch

It's direct, easily understandable. You know what the writer is trying to tell you. Wonderful, isn't it?

Example 3

In reacting to the third paragraph, you very well could have scored it in the (D) or (E) category. Some of the phrases other readers have used to describe their reactions are:

- jargony
- vague and generalized
- no main point
- sounds like a machine wrote it

If you reacted this way, then you as the reader saw this as difficult to read and, though not as convoluted as the first paragraph, in the same ball park.

On the other hand, a few financial analysts who were asked to read this paragraph scored it (A), (B), or (C). They are accustomed to, comfortable with, and skilled at reading this style. The problem is, many people are not.

Example 4

Some common reactions other readers have stated are:

- I had to reread it several times to understand it
- If I had the background for the context, I might understand this better
- boring
- extremely formal
- impersonal

There are a number of problems with this paragraph. In general, the writing is extremely slow-moving. In the first sentence, the writer does not make his point until nearly the end of a 54-word sentence. More often than not, the vocabulary choices cause the reader to linger on the words rather than grasp the writer's meaning and move on. Here are some other examples of elements readers found problematical:

- Unclear terms:

"ongoing effort"—Why not just *effort*?

"appropriate contacts"—Are some contacts inappropriate? Which ones?

"internal" review—Does this mean someone within the company should read them? Who?

"external" comments—Does this mean someone outside the company, such as a consultant, will read them? Who?

- Overly fancy vocabulary choices:
  utilize, acceptability, soliciting, inclusion
- Wordy writing:
  Why "Systems Committee has decided it is necessary"
  rather than simply "Systems Committee decided"?
- Impersonal tone: "it is necessary," "it is also felt"

You may have noted other problems or strengths in these paragraphs. That's fine. The intent here is to help you become increasingly sensitive to what makes writing more or less readable.

2

Gaining Editorial Skill

How Long Should a Sentence Be?

Earlier I mentioned that part of this book's purpose was to help you become more conscious of writing in a way that would be most satisfying to the modern business reader—the reader, you'll recall, who often lacks leisure and patience.

How long should a sentence be? Just as long as a piece of string. There is no hard and fast rule that sentences must be short or long. However, as you may know, shorter sentences are generally preferred by the impatient, busy reader in business today.

Undoubtedly, the greatest influence on business writing today is journalistic style. Journalists and business people are usually writing about the same kinds of content—facts, ideas, and opinions. Journalists and business people are also writing for the same kind of reader—the person "on the run," quickly trying to capture a coherent picture of the events of the moment. Both types of writers also strive to be clear and accurate,* since their readers will undoubtedly use the information they glean from their reading in some way.

Journalists and business writers, therefore, generally strive to write vigorously, concisely, and, most important, clearly, so that the reader will not be misled about the facts and perspective of the story.

Given these goals, in 1946 a man named Rudolf Flesch wrote a book that had a major impact on journalists and, later, on business writers. It was entitled *The Art of Plain Talk* and one of its major tenets was that writers should write short, uncomplicated sentences to improve the readability of their writing. Flesch was not without his critics among journalists. Lester

---

*I am, of course, talking about the highest standards of journalism—not "yellow journalism," which has different goals.

Markel, a former Sunday editor of *The New York Times*, cautioned against short and snappy sentences, maintaining that they "cost something in loss of clarity and perspective."[1]

Nevertheless, Flesch's ideas have been extremely influential, and most journalists and business writers today favor writing shorter sentences.

You will have to make your own decision about this issue. To help you, I'll first give you some guidelines that most good writers, whether in Flesch's camp or some more moderate camp, would endorse. Then you'll have the opportunity to improve the readability of sentences from business reports.

Guidelines for Sentence Length

1. Be careful of very long sentences (more than 18 or 20 words).

....

Example: The company's new management team, after retirement of the former Chairman, has been able to turn Lyson Industries around, resulting in both a substantial working capital and equity cushion and an improved overall debt to equity ratio.

Better: The new management team turned Lyson Industries around after the former Chairman retired. Now working capital and equity are substantial. The debt to equity ratio has also improved.

....

As this example illustrates, you can:

- Break the sentence apart with the comma and the period to achieve *sentences of various lengths*. They add rhythm and emphasis to your prose.

---

[1]Obituary of Dr. Rudolf Flesch, *The New York Times*, October 7, 1986, p. B7.

- Rearrange the sentence and change words to achieve clarity.

2. Be careful of sentences composed of the verb "to be" (is, are, was, were) and a long string of prepositional phrases.

Example: An example *of* financial advisory services *at* Jumbo Bank *is* the provision *of* these services *to* low-income households.

Better: For example, Jumbo Bank provides financial advisory services to low-income households.

When faced with this problem, you can:

- Get rid of the verb *is* and substitute a verb with life in it. You'll usually find that some other word in the sentence contains the root that should be the sentence's main verb (in this case, the word *provision*).
- Rearrange the sentence and eliminate as many prepositions as possible. When you eliminate a preposition, you either get rid of its object or find a new place for the object. Remember, prepositions always have objects: to the *store,* at the *door,* of the *group,* on *time,* etc.

3. Be careful of sentences hooked to other sentences with semicolons, colons, and dashes. These specialized punctuation marks should be used sparingly. The period and the comma should be your major punctuation marks.

Example: Changing financial markets have caused most banks to change their marketing strategies; examples of some of these strategies include: creating a consulting department; targeting medium-sized companies as customers because they are more likely to need consulting services; increasing credit-card services because of their high interest rates; and increasing investment banking transactions which are more profitable.

Better: Banks are selling new products and services because financial markets have changed. One new service is financial consulting to medium-sized companies. Since credit cards carry high interest rates, banks are increasing this line of business. Many are also making highly profitable investment banking deals.

As this example shows you can:

- Break the sentence into sentences of various lengths.
- Add, change, rearrange, or delete words to achieve clarity.
- Punctuate with the comma and the period.

Exercise: Writing Readable Sentences

Here are four unnecessarily long sentences. The thought that is to be communicated is clear. It just takes the reader too much effort to understand it.

Rewrite each sentence so that the thought may be more easily understood.

Your major tools are:

- use of punctuation, primarily the period and comma, to achieve sentences of various lengths.
- eliminating the verb *to be* (is, are, was, were) in sentences where it is accompanied by a string of prepositional phrases.
- adding, changing, rearranging, or deleting words to achieve clarity.

....

1. Although some of us who are familiar with the requested deal have definite reservations about the procedure required, we have to admit that something different has been introduced into the relationship between the customer and his financier which will have a result that as yet we have been unable to predict.

_____

_____

_____

_____

2. Any assistance you require from our Construction Department will be made available upon request if you will just call us at 583–1274; if you have any questions regarding the attached draft as well, please call the same number.

_____

_____

_____

_____

3. The important preparation for Lyco Bank to take prior to the deregulation is in positioning for immediate entry into the new fields of business.

_____

_____

_____

_____

4. We not only have duplications of some tasks under the present system, but each clerk has developed his own work routines and this causes confusion which could be avoided by having a uniform method of processing paperwork.

_____
_____
_____
_____
_____

Suggested Revisions: Writing Readable Sentences

Compare your revisions with these. Keep in mind that these are only *suggestions*. Which do you like better? To what degree does each illustrate the principles we talked about? A number of responses may be possible, and you may come up with better ones than these.

1. Some of us who are familiar with the requested deal have definite reservations about the procedure required. We have to admit, however, that something different has been introduced into the relationship between the customer and his financier. What the ultimate result will be we have not yet been able to predict.

2. If you have any questions about the attached draft or need help from the Construction Department, call 583–1274.

3. Lyco Bank should prepare to enter new fields of business before deregulation occurs.

4. Some tasks are duplicated under the present system and each clerk has developed his own work routines. A uniform method of processing paperwork would eliminate confusion.

Causes and Cures for Wordiness

When you responded earlier to some other people's writing (see pp. 16–19), you probably noticed that several of the paragraphs contained a number of long sentences. You may have indicated that these sentences hindered your ease of reading.

Let's take a look at some of the causes of long sentences. We'll consider the most obvious causes first. They are:

- unnecessary words
- thinking as you write, resulting in repetition or belaboring a point

These problems are sometimes referred to as *wordiness*.

There are two cures for these problems. One is being organized and clear about what you have to say before you write. The other is editing after you write.

It would seem that the first cure is the obvious and appropriate one. Yet even the best writers are not crystal clear about their thoughts when they first sit down to write. Writing is an act of exploration and discovery. We find out what we think as we write.

Thus, for most of us, the first attempt is not the final product. It must be refined, rearranged, clarified—in short, *edited*.

To bring about the second cure, you must become an editor of your own work. This means becoming objective about the presence of wordiness in your writing and not being overly attached to every black mark you put on white paper. It also means taking the time to revise the first draft.

In short, don't worry about being wordy as you write. You may experience "writer's block" if you write and edit simultaneously. But do take the time to edit after you've written.

Learning to edit means recognizing the cause of certain problems and knowing ways to improve or change what's causing the problem.

Perhaps the most common cause of wordiness is unnecessary words. By *unnecessary* I mean words not essential to convey the sentence's meaning clearly.

Unnecessary words come in different guises. The most common offenders are articles (*the, a,* and *an*) and prepositions (*to, for, from, in order to, in addition to, of,* etc.). Other kinds, such as the word *that,* can be determined only in context.

Here's an example of a short, simple sentence that contains unnecessary words:

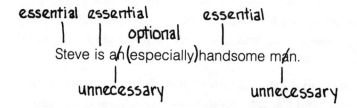

This analysis shows that the article *an* and the noun *man* are not necessary for the thought to be clearly conveyed. *Especially* is a qualifying word that may be necessary to preserve a certain shade of meaning the writer intended.

Thus you might say a sentence contains three classes of words:

Essential words: Those that *must* be written to convey the thought.

Optional words: Those that *may* be used to qualify essential words.

Unnecessary words: Those that you don't need at all because *they say nothing.*

Another type of wordiness comes from the notion that "two words will make the point better than one."

1. Continuing with this project is *useless* and *futile.* (double adjective)

2. The company may *modify* and *change* its business plan. (double verb)

Repetition of this kind does not emphasize the point but merely serves to slow the reader down.

Exercise: Eliminating Unnecessary Words

In these three sentences, find all the unnecessary words you can and *cross them out.* Do not attempt to rearrange the sentences, though some rearrangement might also improve them. Concentrate on simply finding the unnecessary words.

....

1. Smith thinks that the company policy which was designed to cover this matter is obsolete and no longer used.

2. We must not permit ourselves to lose out on these new customers, even if it turns out that we must replace all of their old coffee pots in order to satisfy them.

3. There has been a mishandling of the funds which represents what might be considered inefficiency on the part of the book-keeper and his assistant, although both of them advise that, while the procedure they engaged in is certainly a relatively uncommon one, neither of them sees how his own actions in it can be considered in any way reprehensible or otherwise deserving of censure.

....

Suggested Revisions: Eliminating Unnecessary Words

Notice that I've merely deleted the unnecessary words. No attempt to change the basic sentence structure has been made yet.

1. Smith thinks that the company policy which was designed to cover this matter is obsolete and no longer used.

2. We must not permit ourselves to lose out on these new customers, even if it turns out that we must replace all of their old coffee pots in order.

3. There has been a mishandling of the funds which represents what might be considered inefficiency on the part of the bookkeeper and his assistant, although both of them advise that, while the procedure they engaged in is certainly a (relatively) *optional* uncommon one, neither of them sees how his own actions in it can be considered in any way reprehensible or otherwise deserving of censure.

Repetition and Paragraph Logic

Repetition of words or phrases is not difficult to recognize. Sometimes you must repeat an idea, word, or phrase to be clear. It requires judgment to decide whether repetition makes the writing clearer or detracts from clarity.

Sometimes it's surprising to see how much repetition occurs in a seemingly short and simple piece of writing. A high degree of repetition usually indicates a need for editing.

The *Board of Directors* of the *Company* authorized a *3-for-1 stock split* for *shareholders* of record on June 1, 1988. This *3-for-1 split* is the first *stock split* the *Company* has had in 32 years. A *3-for-1 split* means that 2 additional *shares* will be issued for each *share* held. The *Board of Directors* will publish a *shareholder's* letter next week announcing this *stock split*.

The number of repeated words is amazing, isn't it? This usually results from writing without an organized idea of what you want to say. Thus the logic is unclear.

As a first step toward eliminating some of these repetitions, you have to determine what was wrong with the original plan of organization. That means looking at the pattern of organization the writer chose to see if it will accomplish his or her purpose. In this case, the paragraph was intended to be the opening of a public relations release previewing the stock split.

Here's the main idea of each sentence, summarized:

....

Sentence 1. A split has been authorized.

Sentence 2. It's the first split in 32 years.

Sentence 3. Definition of what a 3-for-1 split means.

Sentence 4. A letter next week will announce the authorization of the stock split.

....

Now ask yourself, is this the right order for the ideas? Given the content of the paragraph, should the ordering of ideas be:

- chronological?
- order of importance?
- comparison and contrast?
- cause and effect analysis?

When writing paragraphs, writers will frequently use one of these methods as a primary way of organizing ideas. Briefly, these patterns and their uses may be described as follows:

Chronological order means observing a time sequence in the ordering of ideas or information.

Use: Content of a historical nature or where it's important to know the sequence of time in which a series of events occurred.

Order of importance means sequencing ideas from most important to least important or the reverse.

Use: *Most important to least important* order is the most common organizational pattern in paragraphs. It's generally clearer to begin with the most important idea and then order illustrations, facts, and explanations logically to amplify the idea.

Least important to most important order is occasionally used to work through a series of facts to a general conclusion that can be inferred from those facts. It's a harder pattern to use because sometimes writers forget to reach a main conclusion.

Comparison and contrast means comparing a group of similarities, a group of differences, or a combination of the two in explaining a general point.

Use: To explore a pattern of similarities or differences as part of a larger analysis.

Cause and effect analysis means explaining why an event had a certain result or how a certain result stemmed from a particular event.

Use: To explore this unique kind of relationship as part of a larger analysis.

Exercise: Revised Order of Importance

Now that you know about these patterns and their uses, reorder the ideas in this paragraph from *most important to least important* order. Keep in mind that the paragraph was intended to be the opening of a public relations release previewing the stock split.

Once again, here's the main idea of each sentence, summarized:

....

Sentence 1. A split has been authorized.

Sentence 2. It's the first split in 32 years.

Sentence 3. Definition of what a 3-for-1 split means.

Sentence 4. A letter next week will announce the authorization of the stock split.

....

Reorder the ideas in most important to least important order:

Most important idea: _____

_____

_____

_____

Next important idea: _____

_____

_____

_____

Next important idea: _____

_____

_____

_____

Least important idea: _____

_____

_____

_____

Suggested Revision: Revised Order of Importance

....

Sentence 1. A split has been authorized.

Sentence 2. A letter next week will announce the authorization of the stock split.

Sentence 3. It's the first split in 32 years.

Sentence 4. Definition of what a 3-for-1 split means.

....

A major problem with the first version is that it seems as though the writer suddenly remembered the existence of the forthcoming announcement letter too late in the writing process and stuck in the last sentence as a kind of afterthought. In terms of priority, however, the publication of the letter "next week" containing the announcement would be more important in a public relations release than a historical fact such as "it is the first split in 32 years." This and the definition of a 3-for-1 split are minor points in comparison to the announcement of the split and the time and means through which the announcement will be made.

When an important point is out of order or stuck in as an afterthought, the writer is clearly disorganized and merely writing as things pop into his mind. The result is invariably *repetitiveness*.

Now using your new order, rewrite the paragraph and eliminate as many repetitions as you can.

Exercise: Eliminating Repetition

The *Board of Directors* of the *Company* authorized a *3-for-1 stock split* for *shareholders* of record on June 1, 1988. This *3-for-1 split* is the first *stock split* the *Company* has had in 32 years. A *3-for-1 split* means that 2 additional *shares* will be issued for each *share* held. The *Board of Directors* will publish a *shareholder's* letter next week announcing this *stock split*.

Revised Order of Importance:

Sentence 1. A split has been authorized.

Sentence 2. A letter next week will announce the authorization of the stock split.

Sentence 3. It's the first split in 32 years.

Sentence 4. Definition of what a 3-for-1 split means.

Your revision: _____

_____

_____

_____

_____

Suggested Revision: Eliminating Repetition

Consider this revision of the paragraph. Once again, this is not the only possible answer. Use it as a guide in assessing your response.

The Board of Directors will publish a letter next week announcing a 3-for-1 stock split for shareholders of record, June 1, 1988. This split, the first in 32 years, means 2 shares will be issued for each one held.

Eliminating Repetition and Belaboring

Repetition and belaboring a point go hand in hand. It's often difficult to separate them clearly in a context, for they stem from the same cause—disorganization.

Three steps used by editors can help you identify and eliminate these problems:

1. Identify all repetitious words and phrases.
2. Identify all sentences that repeat all or part of the same idea.
3. Identify words that are unnecessary.

Exercise: Eliminating Repetition and Belaboring

To help you practice these important skills, read the following paragraph and do three things:

1. Circle all words and short phrases (except pronouns) that are repeated *more than once*. Pronouns will naturally be repeated more often.
2. Circle any parts of sentences or whole sentences that seem to *belabor the same point* unnecessarily.
3. Cross out unnecessary words.

....

1   On June 2, we paid a visit to the Rose Garden Apartment Complex.

2   We met John Smith, the superintendent of the complex. It seems

3   that they have about the same problems as we do, but not on as

4 large a scale, due to the fact that they are a smaller complex.

5 One of their ideas, which is very good, is their security of

6 tenants' keys. They are tagged according to the tenant's

7 Social Security number. This system, we felt, is good because

8 if a key is lost it cannot be traced to the tenant's residence.

9 The system we have now has the tenant's address tagged on the

10 keys. If one of our keys is lost with the tenant's address on

11 it, someone could find the key and we could find ourselves in a

12 very embarrassing position.

....

Suggested Revisions: Eliminating Repetition and Belaboring

....

1 On June 2, we paid a visit to the Rose Garden Apartment Complex.

2 We met John Smith, the superintendent of the complex. It seems

3 that they have about the same problems as we do, but not on as

4 large a scale, due to the fact that they are a smaller complex.

5 One of their ideas, which is very good, is their security of

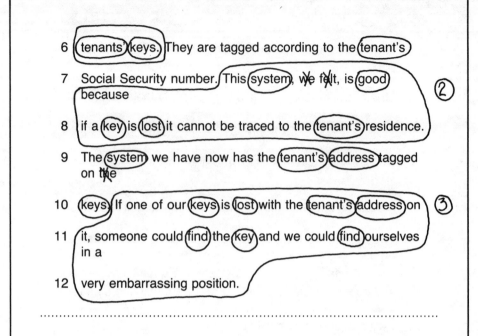

6 tenants' keys. They are tagged according to the tenant's

7 Social Security number. This system, we felt, is good because

8 if a key is lost it cannot be traced to the tenant's residence.

9 The system we have now has the tenant's address tagged on the

10 keys. If one of our keys is lost with the tenant's address on

11 it, someone could find the key and we could find ourselves in a

12 very embarrassing position.

Commentary: Eliminating Repetition and Belaboring

Compare your answer to this one. You probably caught most of the repeated words. Again, the number is staggering.

Surprisingly, there are not too many words you can cross out without creating nonsentences. However, if you had been allowed to rearrange and combine sentences, you could probably have eliminated lots of excess words.

The belabored point occurs in three sentences: lines 5–6, 7–8 and 10–12. These three sentences are basically saying all or part of the same idea:

Tagging tenants' keys with their Social Security numbers rather than their address is a good idea because if the key is lost it cannot be traced back to the owner's residence.

Exercise: Combining Editorial Techniques

Once you have done these three editorial steps, you are ready to "clean up." Assume that the logic is okay. This time, rearrange and combine sentences as much as you like. You should be able to eliminate a lot of repetition and wordiness.

....

1   On June 2, we paid a visit to the Rose Garden Apartment Complex.

2   We met John Smith, the superintendent of the complex. It seems

3   that they have about the same problems as we do, but not on as

4   large a scale, due to the fact that they are a smaller complex.

5   One of their ideas, which is very good, is their security of

6   tenants' keys. They are tagged according to the tenant's

7   Social Security number. This system, we felt, is good because

8   if a key is lost it cannot be traced to the tenant's residence.

9   The system we have now has the tenant's address tagged on the

10   keys. If one of our keys is lost with the tenant's address on

11   it, someone could find the key and we could find ourselves in a

12   very embarrassing position.

Your revision:_____

_____

_____

_____

_____

....

Suggested Revision: Combining Editorial Techniques

Compare your revision to this one. Obviously it is only one of many possible versions. The point is to eliminate the large number of repetitions and keep the basic message intact. If your version does this, it's fine.

....

1 ~~On June 2,~~ We ~~paid a visit~~ visited to the Rose Garden Apartment Complex, on June 2 and

2 We met John Smith, the complex's superintendent. ~~of the complex. It seems~~

3 ~~that~~ They have about the same problems ~~as~~ we do, but ~~not~~ on ~~as a~~ smaller

4 ~~large a~~ scale, ~~due to the fact that~~ because they are a smaller complex.

5 One ~~of their ideas, which is~~ very good idea, is their security of

6 tenants' keys. ~~They~~ which are tagged ~~according~~ by ~~to the tenant's~~

7 Social Security number. ~~This system, we felt, is good because~~

8 ~~if a key is lost it cannot be traced to the tenant's residence.~~

9 ~~The system~~ We have ~~now has~~ the tenant's address tagged on ~~the~~

10   keys. If one ~~of our keys~~ is lost ~~with the tenant's address on~~

11   ~~it,~~ someone could find ~~the key~~ and we could ~~find ourselves~~
         it   *be*
     in ~~a~~

                    trouble.
12   ~~very embarrassing position.~~

....

Here is the above revision reprinted:

....

We visited the Rose Garden Apartment Complex on June 2
and met John Smith, the Complex's superintendent. They
have about the same problems we do, but on a smaller
scale, because they are a smaller complex. One very good
idea is their security of tenants' keys, which are tagged by
Social Security number. We have the tenant's address
tagged on keys. If one is lost, someone could find it and we
could be in trouble.

....

3

Active versus Passive Voice

Recognizing Active and Passive Voices

Read these two paragraphs on the same subject. Be aware of the degrees of wordiness in each and the effect of the wordiness on you as a reader.

....

Example 1

Dear Congressman:

Your assistance in utilizing both congressional and appropriate Government office pressure to bring an end to the PATH strike, now in its 53rd day, would be sincerely welcomed by both your constituents and those constituents of other members of the New Jersey Congressional Delegation. The very fact that 80,000 New Jersey commuters have been seriously inconvenienced for this long space of time indicates the vital necessity of Government intervention. The New York subway strike was settled in a minimum amount of time, whereas the PATH strike has not received the attention of any Governmental organization. For your information the additional expense of commuting via bus and New York City subway has increased my commuting expense to $105.00 monthly, an intolerable burden.

....

Example 2

Dear Congressman:

Your constituents need you to bring pressure to end the PATH strike. The New York City Government settled its strike quickly, but no Governmental organization in New Jersey has paid any attention to the PATH strike. I, like 80,000 other New Jersey commuters, am very upset. I now pay $105.00 a month in commuting expenses, an intolerable burden.

....

By now, you have become much more sensitive to writing that is readable, and you probably recognized that the second paragraph speaks more directly to you. Nice, isn't it? It more readily captures your attention than the first. In this case—where the writer wanted action on the PATH strike—getting the Congressman's attention was probably a good idea.

A major difference between these two paragraphs is that the first is written mostly in passive voice while the second is written in active voice.

Active voice basically means that the words of the sentence are lined up in a certain order:

actor	action	*indirect receiver of action*	*direct receiver of action*
Eve	gave	Adam	the apple.

Most English sentences fall into this pattern. It's direct. We know who the main "actor" of the sentence is (Eve, in this case), what she did and to whom.

Since this pattern is so common and natural to the language, it is sometimes also called "normal word order."

Passive voice *reverses* the normal word order of the active sentence.

object becomes subject of sentence	action	*actor becomes object of prepositional phrase*
The apple	was given	by Eve

indirect receiver of action becomes object of prepositional phrase

to Adam.

Notice that the emphasis of the passive sentence changes. Our focus is on *the apple* rather than on Eve. The phrase *by Eve* could even be omitted, and often is.

....

The apple was given to Adam.

....

Now we've totally lost sight of the subject of the original sentence—Eve, the vital "actor" in that scenario. Some Biblical scholars would argue that it's *the apple* that's really the important point in the story. Not Eve. The apple symbolizes "Original Sin."

Other scholars, of course, would argue that Adam's carnal attraction to Eve symbolizes man's hopeless estrangement from God and spirituality. Thus Eve is more important than the apple.

Your scholarly point of view, in this case, would probably decide whether you would write the sentence in active or passive voice.

Why have I taken what might appear to be a nit-picking digression? Because it's *where you want readers to focus their attention* that ultimately determines whether a sentence is written in active or passive voice.

A type of passive phrasing related to passive voice is called an *expletive*. Here's an example:

....

It was observed in the Garden of Eden that Eve gave Adam the apple.

or

There is a story that Eve gave the apple to Adam.

....

Expletives, like passive voice, shift the sentence's emphasis from the subject (Eve, in this case) to a meaningless phrase ("It was observed," "There is"). And, like passive voice, expletives lengthen the sentence.

Most of the time, business writers should use active voice. It's more direct because it is the normal way we think and talk. Passive sentences are also longer and more wordy than active sentences, as our simple example about Adam and Eve illustrates.

However, as our little illustration also shows, it's important for writers to use active voice *when they wish to* and passive voice *when they wish to*.

Before this can happen, you must recognize easily when a verb is in active voice and when it's in passive voice. Let's examine this issue first.

Exercise: Recognizing Active and Passive Sentences

You will find below ten sentences. Indicate whether they are active or passive by putting "A" or "P" in the line provided. Refer back to the definition examples if you need to.

....

1. The accountant made an error in his calculations. _____
2. The check was given to John three days late. _____
3. Your contribution will be appreciated. _____
4. Economies of scale were closely observed by the company. _____
5. The company's economies of scale contributed to its bottom-line profit. _____
6. Your interest in my résumé is greatly appreciated. _____
7. I recommend that we offer this company a line of credit. _____

8. The Vice President took charge of the company's overseas operation. _____
9. It was noted that the committee gave its recommendations on the project. _____
10. The boxer was knocked out by his opponent. _____

Answers: Recognizing Active and Passive Sentences

1. The accountant made an error in his calculations. __A__
2. The check was given to John three days late. __P__
3. Your contribution will be appreciated. __P__
4. Economies of scale were closely observed by the company. __P__
5. The company's economies of scale contributed to its bottom-line profit. __A__
6. Your interest in my résumé is greatly appreciated. __P__
7. I recommend that we offer this company a line of credit. __A__
8. The Vice President took charge of the company's overseas operation. __A__
9. It was noted that the committee gave its recommendations on the project. __P (expletive)__
10. The boxer was knocked out by his opponent. __P__

The Habit of Passive Writing

It's easy to recognize active and passive voice when isolated examples are shown. Now try the following paragraph.

Exercise: Recognizing Passive Verbs

Underline all the verbs that you think are passive.

1 The International Monetary System that prevailed

2 in the postwar period until 1971 was conceived at

3 the Bretton Woods Conference of 1944. Monetary

4 experts had two major objectives. First, it was

5 hoped that they could create a system that would

6 eliminate the worst features of the system that

7 prevailed during the interwar period, especially

8 devices such as competitive exchange devaluations

9 and exchange controls. (These two devices had been

10 resorted to by most of the major economies of the

11 world in an attempt to increase employment and reverse

12 the economic decline of the depression.) Second,

13 it was desired that the system would allow countries

14 to have a degree of independence in pursuing domestic

15 economic policy. It can be recalled from the previous

16 section of this module that fixed exchange rates, if

17 rigidly enforced, can lead to domestic unemployment

18 and other unwanted internal effects.

Answers: Recognizing Passive Verbs

The passage contains *five* passive verbs:

....

1   The International Monetary System that prevailed

                        (1)

2   in the postwar period until 1971 *was conceived* at

3   the Bretton Woods Conference of 1944. Monetary

4   experts had two major objectives. First, *it was*

    (2)

5   *hoped* that they could create a system that would

6   eliminate the worst features of the system that

7   prevailed during the interwar period, especially

8   devices such as competitive exchange devaluations

9   and exchange controls. (These two devices *had been*

    (3)

10 *resorted to* by most of the major economies of the

11 world in an attempt to increase employment and reverse

12 the economic decline of the depression. Second,

    (4)

13 *it was desired* that the system would allow countries

14 to have a degree of independence in pursuing domestic

    (5)

15 economic policy. *It can be recalled* from the previous

16 section of this module that fixed exchange rates, if

17 rigidly enforced, can lead to domestic unemployment

18 and other unwanted internal effects.

....

This passage illustrates what frequently happens when the writer begins to write in passive voice. Whole paragraphs and, indeed, whole sections of a report are frequently written totally with passive sentences, expletives, and verbs of being (*is, was, were*), which also express no action.

I can only guess at the reasons for this "habit of passive writing." What probably happens is that once writers put their feet on the path of passive sentence structure, they unconsciously become fully committed to the inverted patterns and longer length of passive sentences. In fact, their ears may hear these longer rhythms as more "elegant" than the shorter, staccato rhythms of active sentences.

Another contributing element to consistently passive writing may be the dim memory most people have of being told by their English teacher to keep their tenses (past, present, future) consistent in a paragraph. There's no rule, however, that says voice must be consistent in a paragraph. Do not confuse the two.

I think you can see from these examples that a large-scale use of passive voice lengthens sentences, increases wordiness, and makes understanding the message more difficult.

Exercise: Eliminating the Passive

Now you'll have the opportunity to rewrite this paragraph in active voice. Be especially conscious of improving the *clarity* and *readability* of the writing. For example, if a prepositional phrase has been dropped and you can *infer from context* what its object would have been, decide whether or not making that object the subject of the new active sentence would improve clarity and readability.

1   The International Monetary System that prevailed
                                    (1)
2   in the postwar period until 1971 *was conceived* at

3   the Bretton Woods Conference of 1944. Monetary

4   experts had two major objectives. First, *it was*
        (2)
5   *hoped* that they could create a system that would

6   eliminate the worst features of the system that

7   prevailed during the interwar period, especially

8   devices such as competitive exchange devaluations

9   and exchange controls. (These two devices *had been*
        (3)
10   *resorted to* by most of the major economies of the

11   world in an attempt to increase employment and reverse

12   the economic decline of the depression.) Second,
        (4)
13   *it was desired* that the system would allow countries

14   to have a degree of independence in pursuing domestic
                                    (5)
15   economic policy. *It can be recalled* from the previous

16   section of this module that fixed exchange rates, if

17   rigidly enforced, can lead to domestic unemployment

18   and other unwanted internal effects.

Your revision: _____

_____

_____

_____

_____

_____

_____

_____

_____

_____

_____

_____

_____

_____

_____

_____

_____

_____

_____

_____

_____

_____

_____

_____

_____

Suggested Revision: Eliminating the Passive

1 Monetary experts *conceived* [^(1)] the International Monetary

2 System at the Bretton Woods Conference in 1944. They

3 had two major objectives. First, they *hoped* [^(2)] they could

4 create a system that would eliminate the worst

5   features of the system that prevailed during the

6   interwar period, especially devices such as

7   competitive exchange devaluations and exchange

8   controls. (Most of the major economies of the world

9   *had resorted* (3) to these two devices in an attempt to in-

10 crease employment and reverse the decline of the

11 depression.) Second, they *desired* (4) that the system

12 would allow countries to have a degree of independence

13 in pursuing domestic economic policy. You *may recall* (5)

14 from the previous section of this module that fixed

15 exchange rates, if rigidly enforced, can lead to

16 domestic unemployment and other unwanted internal

17 effects.

....

Commentary: Eliminating the Passive

Notice that the editor inferred from context what the subjects of the active sentences should be for examples 1, 4, and 5. In example 5, you had to figure out that the paragraph is from a reading such as a textbook (the word "module" is a clue). The subject of the last sentence could also be written "The reader may recall." This would not, however, be as direct as the construction "You may recall."

In all five cases, using active voice improves the clarity and directness of the sentences. If active voice had been used together with some of the other techniques you've studied, the sentences could have been improved even more.

As we've already discussed, however, there is no law that says you must use active voice as opposed to passive voice. The choice is made on the basis of your purpose in the sentence or paragraph.

To Use or Not to Use Passive Voice

Most business writers prefer the normal word order of active voice. Sometimes, however, they will prefer to use passive voice. Why?

Passive voice is a better choice in business writing when:

1. You *truly* need to be tactful and must omit who did something—you're not merely covering yourself.
2. You want to focus on an idea rather than on the person who had the idea (usually yourself).
3. You must write "politically." For example, you are writing to a "hostile" reader who is more powerful than you in the company.

Some examples will clarify these points.

....

Tactfulness

Passive: Journal entry errors were made in the books.

Active: Our accountant made journal entry errors in the books.

....

If there's no need to make trouble for the accountant, then you would probably choose the passive sentence.

Content Focus

Passive: A secured loan will be offered to the customer.

Active: I will offer the customer a secured loan.

If it's important to identify who will offer the loan (yourself, in this case), you'll choose active voice. If it isn't—if, for example, the sentence is part of an internal memo at the bank and it's clear who is making the offer—you'll probably use passive voice.

Political Writing

Passive: Several objections have been raised as a result of some points made at the last task-force meeting.

Active: The task-force members raised several objections to your points made at the last meeting.

If your objective is basically to slow down the reader's comprehension of negative or sensitive issues, then you'll use the passive. In this example, the first sentence (in passive voice) omits the source of the objections while the active sentence highlights the source. If the reader has power over the task force members and could make trouble for them, it makes sense to raise objections to his or her ideas carefully and slowly.

A word of warning about political writing. Some business writers write as if every report, letter, and proposal is a volatile political situation. Thus their style is always passive, circumlocutive, and turgid. I believe such a habit is unnecessary; surely every writing situation we face on our jobs is not fraught with political danger.

Exercise: Passive or Active?

In each of these pairs of sentences, one is active and one is passive.

First, put an "A" next to the active sentence and a "P" next to the passive sentence.

Then, identify in the space provided which voice you would use for the particular reader or readers described and briefly explain why.

....

    1. Profits were increased by Burco Inc. in 1986. _____
    2. Burco Inc. increased its profits in 1986. _____

....

Which voice would you use for:

A report to a current investor thinking of buying Burco stock?

_____ Voice

Why?_____

_____

_____

_____

_____

A report to current stockholders?

_____ Voice

Why?_____

_____

_____

_____

_____

3. The task force has recommended an early retirement program for all members of the company. _____
4. An early retirement program has been recommended for all company employees. _____

Which voice would you use for:

A notice to all employees of the company announcing a change in retirement benefits?

_____ Voice

Why?_____

_____

_____

_____

_____

5. I urge all company employees to contribute as much as possible to this worthy cause. _____
6. All company employees are urged to contribute as much as possible to this worthy cause. _____

Which voice would you use for:

A memorandum sent companywide to promote the "worthy cause" and signed by you. (You are probably a high-ranking officer of the corporation.)

_____ Voice

Why?_____

_____

_____

_____

_____

A memorandum sent to members of your team since you've been appointed team chairman of the "worthy cause."

_____ Voice

Why?_____

_____

_____

_____

_____

. . . .

7. Your tax return must be completed by April 15. _____
8. You must complete your tax return by April 15. _____

. . . .

Which voice would you use for:

A letter in which this sentence is part of a series of instructions to taxpayers from the IRS specifying procedures and deadlines for the completion of tax returns.

_____ Voice

Why?_____

_____

_____

_____

_____

....

    9. A more concise presentation of ideas needs to be orga-
nized for our next meeting. _____

   10. Please organize your ideas and present them more concisely at our next meeting. _____

....

Which voice would you use when:

You're the boss writing to a group of your employees. You're
trying to get them to be more responsive at meetings without wasting everyone's time by long-winded speeches.

_____ Voice

Why?_____

_____

_____

_____

_____

You're an employee with a long-winded boss. In a follow-up
report on a meeting you had with him, you're trying to plant
the seed of the idea that he needs to be more organized in
his meetings with you.

_____ Voice

Why?_____
_____
_____
_____
_____

Commentary: Passive or Active?

....

    1. Profits were increased by Burco Inc. in 1986. __P__
    2. Burco Inc. increased its profits in 1986. __A__

....

Which voice would you use for:

A report to a current investor thinking of buying Burco stock.

Active Voice

Why? The emphasis in the active sentence is on Burco as the generator of increased profits. Burco's ability to make profits would be of primary interest to someone thinking of investing in the company's stock.

A report to current stockholders.

Passive Voice

Why? Current stockholders have already committed themselves to Burco and are interested in the return they can expect on their investment.

....

    3. The task force has recommended an early retirement program for all members of the company. __A__
    4. An early retirement program has been recommended for all company employees. __P__

....

Which voice would you use for:

A notice to all employees of the company announcing a change in retirement benefits.

Passive Voice

Why? Employees would be interested in the content of the recommendation, not the group that made it.

....

5. I urge all company employees to contribute as much as possible to this worthy cause. __A__

6. All company employees are urged to contribute as much as possible to this worthy cause. __P__

....

Which voice would you use for:

A memorandum sent companywide to promote the "worthy cause" and signed by you. (You are probably a high-ranking officer of the Corporation).

Active Voice

Why? You want your name associated with the cause in people's minds. This association is likely to prompt them to contribute.

A memorandum sent to members of your team since you've been appointed team chairman of the "worthy cause."

Passive Voice

Why? Your role as the one urging people to give money does not add additional value to the cause in their minds. In fact, your association with the cause might be negative for some people, who prefer not to be told what charities to give to. You may not want to be thought of as one who tells others where to make charitable contributions.

....

7. Your tax return must be completed by April 15. __P__

8. You must complete your tax return by April 15. __A__

....

Which voice would you use for:

A letter in which this sentence is part of a series of instructions to taxpayers from the IRS specifying procedures and deadlines for the completion of tax returns.

Passive Voice

Why? You want to focus the reader on completing the return before the deadline. The reader may choose to have his accountant complete the return. The active statement "*You* must complete . . . " is therefore misleading.

....

9. A more concise presentation of ideas needs to be organized for our next meeting. __P__

10. Please organize your ideas and present them concisely at our next meeting. __A__

....

Which voice would you use when:

You're the boss writing to a group of your employees. You're trying to get them to be more responsive at meetings without wasting everyone's time by long-winded speeches.

Active Voice

Why? You're a superior writing to subordinates and, in a polite way, admonishing them to "shape up."

You're an employee with a long-winded boss. In a follow-up report on a meeting you had with him, you're trying to plant the seed of the idea that he needs to be more organized in his meetings with you.

Passive Voice

Why? You're a subordinate writing to a superior. You need to be tactful about pointing out a weakness of his (or hers).

4

Purpose and Vocabulary

Becoming Sensitive to Words

Here's some good news and some bad news about English. The good news is: the English language contains an enormous number of words. It is one of the most expressive vocabularies in the world. The bad news is: this richness of opportunity allows so many choices that clarity and tonal appropriateness are often sacrificed for some other intent.

Purpose determines word choice. In polemical writing, such as Germaine Greer's or John Milton's, the writer's purpose is to express herself or himself, to persuade. In literary writing, such as a descriptive passage in a novel or a poem, the writer wants to express moods, feelings, or other subjective states of mind. In a discussion of a theory from physics, the purpose is to explain a highly abstract concept or principle.

In business writing, the purpose is generally clear, direct communication of noncontroversial, factual subjects. It is probably closest in purpose and, therefore, in tone and style to expository writing such as the excerpt you saw from the book on the new tax laws. People may write "I feel" a lot in business, but they're really talking about ideas and facts, not feelings. Ideas and facts are what you use to explain something.

Achieving an appropriate tone is just as important in business writing as in other kinds of writing. Tone comes primarily from words. The most basic tool any good writer needs is sensitivity to words.

Sensitivity to words first means knowing what they mean. Words have two kinds of meanings—denotative and connotative. *Denotation* is the precise meaning a word carries—what you might think of as the "dictionary definition." *Connotation* is the feelings and imagery a word evokes—what you might think of as its "associated meanings."

For example, all these words basically mean, or *denote,* the same thing:

- drunk
- intoxicated
- inebriated
- tipsy
- soused

The connotations are different, however. Being *tipsy* is thought of as a milder and more jovial form of drunkenness than being *intoxicated* or *inebriated. Drunk* is probably the most neutral and objective term, while *soused* carries the connotation of being drunk in a disorderly, falling-down sort of way. It's the connotations of these words that determine how you use them.

Some words are used primarily for their denotative meaning, which is precise and specialized: for example, jargon and words derived from Greek, Old French, or Latin roots. Other words have such abstract meanings that they must be combined with examples or more concrete vocabulary to come really clear in the context.

To use any word effectively, you must be sensitive to its strengths and limitations. It all boils down to being interested enough in words themselves to consider why you're making one choice over another.

The most important and easily accessible tool writers have for choosing words appropriately is their dictionary. A good dictionary will define the denotative and, oftentimes, the connotative meanings of words. The most fundamental error a writer can make is choosing a word that doesn't mean what he thinks it does. The more specialized the word is or the more richly connotative it is, the easier it is to be mistaken about its meaning.

Exercise: Connotation and Denotation

The writers of the following sentences probably failed to check their dictionary. You're going to have the opportunity now to improve their word choice. Read each sentence and explain why the italicized words carry the wrong connotation or denotation for the context. In each case, supply a more appropriate word. If you have problems, by all means use your dictionary.

1. We wanted to have our office party at Gregory's, but our boss *negated* the idea.
   Problem with word choice:_____
   More appropriate word: _____

2. I am pleased with the *drastic* improvement in your tardiness record over the last few weeks.
   Problem with word choice:_____
   More appropriate word: _____

3. Return on sales *experienced* a considerable increase over the five-year historical period studied.
   Problem with word choice:_____
   More appropriate word: _____

4. The company must *enhance* its sales by opening new retail outlets in areas where it has never done business before.
   Problem with word choice:_____
   More appropriate word: _____

5. The new advertising program is *merely* intended to provide the company with a whole new image.
   Problem with word choice:_____
   More appropriate word: _____

6. I would find it *pleasurable* to be of service to you.
   Problem with word choice:_____
   More appropriate word: _____

7. That was a very *crafty* proposal you made.
   Problem with word choice:_____
   More appropriate word: _____

8. It was truly a pleasure having my first personal *interaction* at Largo Company with such an intelligent and dynamic person as you.

Problem with word choice:_____

More appropriate word: _____

Suggested Revisions: Connotation and Denotation

1. We wanted to have our office party at Gregory's, but our boss *negated* the idea.

Problem with word choice: Wrong word altogether. *Negated* means to nullify or deny the truth of.

More appropriate word: *opposed, objected to, rejected*

2. I am pleased with the *drastic* improvement in your tardiness record over the last few weeks.

Problem with word choice: *Drastic* means *harsh*, *rigorous*, or *severe*, as in *drastic* punishment.

More appropriate word: *noticeable* or *dramatic*

3. Return on sales *experienced* a considerable increase over the five-year historical period studied.

Problem with word choice: People *experience* things, but ratios do not.

More appropriate word: *increased, went up*

4. The company must *enhance* sales by opening new retail outlets in areas where it has never done business before.

Problem with word choice: *Enhance* means to raise to a higher degree or to raise the value or price of. The sentence seems to be talking about increasing sales by opening more stores.

More appropriate word: *increase, make more*

5. The new advertising program is *merely* intended to provide the company with a whole new image.

Problem with word choice: *Merely* means "only as specified, and nothing more," as in "merely as a matter of form." The context clearly calls for a different word.

More appropriate word: *primarily*, *mainly*, or just eliminate merely

6. I would find it *pleasurable* to be of service to you.

   Problem with word choice: The adjective *pleasurable* derives from the noun *pleasure,* which connotes strong physical sensations or strong feelings of joy or delight. All these connotations seem inappropriate for this context.

   More appropriate word: *enjoyable, be pleased,* or *be glad*

7. That was a very *crafty* proposal you made.

   Problem with word choice: *Crafty* connotes being shrewd in a *deceitful* way. (In some cases, of course, this could be the right word.)

   More appropriate word: *shrewd, clever*

8. It was truly a pleasure having my first personal *interaction* at Largo Company with such an intelligent and dynamic person as you.

   Problem with word choice: Interaction means "mutual action or influence." It's too abstract for this context.

   More appropriate word: *meeting, contact, visit*

The Problem with Abstract Words

Some people find it difficult to be practical and down to earth in their business writing. Their writing is always straining toward the lofty realm of the abstract, just out of reach of the reader's clear comprehension.

Examples

The recession will gain momentum and impact the company's cyclical ventures.

A clear vision as manifested in a direct objective shared by all within an organization is paramount in a dynamic, complex environment.

To the extent that an entity does not affect the dynamics of its environment, the appropriate response to change will necessarily be dictated by the environment. The essence of operating in a complex marketplace is not to adapt but rather to become adaptable on an ongoing basis.

Most people speak easily in direct, concrete terms and examples. In general, we think in concrete particulars more easily than in abstract ideas. After all, our everyday lives are made up of millions of concrete actions—buying the newspaper, opening the front door, cooking dinner, etc.

Thus the tendency to write abstractly is not the result of a primary tendency to speak and think this way. Yet when people put their thoughts on paper, abstractions often abound.

There are basically two motivations behind a tendency to favor abstract words in writing. One is a conscious motive. People want to be precise rather than misleading.

When trying to be precise, people are often "all-inclusive." This means attempting to define the total universe in which something might take place.

For example, consider the sentence "We are taking precautions against fire." The word *precautions* is all-inclusive. It may be used to indicate many things that are being done. It may be used to indicate some things that are being done and others that will be done (but are not yet known). But the word does not define *exactly* what will be done—it gives only a general idea of the total universe of possible fire precautions. However, if you write, "We are installing fire doors and an automatic sprinkler system," the reader knows precisely what will be done.

In addition, defining the total universe of something suggests theoretical discourse to many people. Explaining theories requires the use of abstract vocabulary because these kinds of words are necessary to explain and define the world of ideas. But little of what is written in the everyday, mundane world of business really qualifies as "theoretical."

A second motive—a less-conscious one—stems from a self-protective instinct. Whenever people put words on paper, they know they are going to last. Unlike spoken words, which have a life of a brief moment and can be changed by simply saying, "What I said was" or "That's not what I said," written words are not easily erased. In particular, report writers, who are anticipating a response from their reader, consider what reactions and attacks may be engendered by their writing.

These "attacks" come in different forms.

- "Why didn't you . . . ."
- "Did you investigate . . . ."
- "Did you think of . . . ."
- "What about . . . ."

A sinking feeling comes over most business writers when they contemplate such responses.

Fear of such responses is not a case of paranoia. It is based in reality. History provides a lengthy record of people's writings being attacked and the consequences that ensued to the writer. One can think of many examples—Martin Luther (when he nailed the 95 theses to the church door), Galileo's revolutionary theories, and Freud's writings.

Think back to many of your college and high school courses. Didn't they often involve a critique of someone's ideas through his or her writing? And of course, receiving a grade on a written paper or examination always meant receiving a critique of your written ideas.

The way to protect oneself from professors' critiques, as most students readily learn, is to become more abstract and, therefore, harder to pin down on any specific points (or potential errors).

This self-protective mechanism works for self-protection. It does not, however, aid clear communication. Self-protection must ultimately be sacrificed if you want to be clear about communicating what you think. Martin Luther, Galileo, and Freud knew this and undoubtedly braced themselves for the consequences. But they were more concerned to communicate a new idea to the world than to protect themselves. I doubt that any of you will be called upon to die for your ideas. Yet everyone knows that the power of the written word is enormous. These subliminal realizations often call up business writers' protective mechanisms when they must go "on the record."

Let's take again the example, "We are taking precautions against fire." If somebody writes specifically, "We are installing fire doors and an automatic sprinkler system," he may be concerned that somebody else will say, "And what about smoke detectors?" So he writes instead, "We are taking precautions against fire."

Not only do people fear attack from those who disagree with them. What about their friends? How many people fear the so-called "well-meaning criticism" of friends, bosses, and teachers playing devil's advocate against their ideas? There's a well-worn, trite, but true saying: With friends like this, who needs enemies?

In no way, of course, am I implying that you should, could, or would want to write without abstract words. But you must combine them properly with concrete words and examples.

Definitions are a precise blend of the abstract and the concrete. Think for a moment about how you might define a pen.

Some of the phrases that may have come to your mind are:

- my pen is blue
- long, thin instrument
- writing instrument
- uses ink
- ballpoint or fountain

Of course, all of these can be challenged. *Long* and *thin* could also describe a toothbrush. A writing instrument could be a pencil. A rubber stamp uses ink. Pencils can be blue. "Ballpoint" or "fountain" describes specific types of pens.

As you may have already guessed, part of defining something is to put it into an abstract category.

A pen is a *writing instrument*.

But this alone does not define a pen. The description must also be concrete.

A pen is a *long, thin* writing instrument that *uses ink*.

Combining the abstract category and the specific descriptions yields a satisfying definition of a pen.

Thus the issue in good writing, especially report writing, is achieving the needed balance among abstract words, concrete words, and examples to communicate points clearly and completely.

I am assuming that your objective in business writing will generally *not* be to be purposefully unclear, as dictators, demagogues, and some politicians are. Such writers and speakers have basically dishonest motives behind the profusion of abstract words that they throw at the reader or listener. I can deal only with the motivations I've already discussed, which are basically honest, though not always necessary.

Exercise: Blending Abstract and Concrete

Blending the abstract and the concrete requires three kinds of knowledge:

- of your subject
- of your message
- of words

Not all abstract words should be eliminated. But if a passage has too many abstract terms at the expense of concrete words and examples, the readers may not understand the message, may interpret it incorrectly, or may simply "turn off."

Following you will find three paragraphs, one about buying a car, one about gardening, and the third about music.

Pick the paragraph that interests you most. Then list the abstract words in the spaces provided.

....

Buying a Car

It is important to be aware of quality when choosing a personal vehicle. A vehicle is seen as most valuable when it reflects lifestyle and personality. Reliability, maintenance, and dependability are also considered significant factors.

List all the abstract words you can find in this paragraph._____

_____

_____

_____

_____

....

The Joys of Gardening

Gardening is a very satisfying activity. The most enjoyable part is the maintenance of the garden. The physical activity required is very healthy. It's also invigorating to be out of doors and experience your environment.

List all the abstract words you can find in this paragraph._____

_____

_____

_____

_____

Listening to Music

People generally listen to music that they think expresses their personality. Thus some people like rock, some like jazz, and some like classical. There are vastly different moods and world views embodied in these three styles. Some people think each of these types of music speaks a different language to the listener.

List all the abstract words you can find in this paragraph._____

_____

_____

_____

_____

Here is a list of the abstract words.

Buying a Car

quality	personality
vehicle	reliability
valuable	maintenance
reflects	dependability
lifestyle	significant factors

The Joys of Gardening

activity	healthy
maintenance	experience
physical activity	environment

Listening to Music

expresses	world views
personality	embodied
rock	styles
jazz	types
classical	language
moods	

Once again, choose one of the three paragraphs that interests you most. Then, for the italicized abstract words, substitute words or examples that would, in the context, make the writing more concrete. (You may, of course, revise all three paragraphs.)

Using an example from *Buying a Car*, here's how I would make the abstraction, *lifestyle*, more concrete.

....

People who think of themselves as "success stories" but also "free spirits" often drive sports cars as part of their lifestyle. The moderately wealthy adventurer might choose a Corvette or perhaps a Firebird. But for most people I know, the symbol of total success and total freedom remains the Porsche.

....

I substituted words and examples that come from my experience of buying a car. Your revision will come from your experience.

Rewrite the italicized abstractions in the paragraph of your choice.

....

Buying a Car

It is important to be aware of *quality* when choosing a personal *vehicle*. A *vehicle* is seen as most valuable when it reflects lifestyle and personality. Reliability, maintenance, and dependability are also considered significant factors.

Your revision: _____

_____

_____

_____

_____

....

The Joys of Gardening

Gardening is a very satisfying *activity*. The most enjoyable part is the *maintenance* of the garden. The physical activity required is very healthy. It's also invigorating to be out of doors and *experience* your environment.

Your revision: _____

_____

_____

_____

_____

....

Listening to Music

People generally listen to music that they think expresses their personality. Thus some people like rock, some like jazz, and some like classical. There are vastly different *moods* and world views *embodied* in these three styles. Some people think each of these types of music speaks a different *language* to the listener.

Your revision: _____

_____

_____

_____

_____

Suggested Revisions: Blending Abstract and Concrete

Here are some sample revisions. Yours will undoubtedly be different and may be better. Make sure you have achieved a good blend of the abstract and the concrete.

Buying a Car

It is important to be aware of quality when choosing a personal vehicle. Whether it's a jeep, moped, skateboard, or Ferrari, you don't want it to break down and leave you stranded on a dark road at night. You also want your vehicle to express your personality. The free spirits who like the wind in their hair prefer the free-wheeling style of a convertible. After all, aren't skateboards and mopeds just a form of convertible?

The Joys of Gardening

Gardening is very satisfying to the senses. When you dig and hoe the earth to prepare it to receive seeds or bulbs, you touch it, smell it, and feel it. It's invigorating to smell clay and lime. Dig deeper and you may feel the slimy touch of an earthworm before you see its almost transparent form blending with the earth. The final sensory pleasure is the vibrant gold of a jonquil bed or the piquant taste of a radish.

....

Listening to Music

People generally listen to the music they believe expresses their personality. For example, jazz is sometimes called "sexual music" because of its hard-driving beat and sensual harmonies. The word *jazz*, in fact, originally meant "to have sex." It may be no accident that real jazz is rarely heard outside of dark, smoke-filled clubs where assignations are the general rule.

(Note that only one example—jazz—is treated here.)

....

5

Straight Talk

"Elegant" Words

When William the Conqueror conquered England in 1066, the English language was changed forever. For generations after the Norman Conquest, the most important political and social positions in England were held by French-speaking Normans. Writing, which was usually done by churchmen, was done in Latin. And the "people" spoke old English ("Englisc"), a fusion of Saxon, Viking, and Danish languages.

Old English reflected the everyday life of an agricultural people. Our modern English is impossible without this vocabulary. Computer analysis has shown that the one hundred most common words in English—words such as *the, you, what, that*—are Anglo-Saxon.[1]

The aristocrats carried on the "higher" activities of society—religion, law, science, and literature—in French or Latin. Latin was primarily the language of religion and learning, while French was spoken in "high society."

From the mingling of these three languages—Old English, Latin, and Old French—modern English developed its enormous vocabulary and its ability to express different shades of meaning and fine distinctions.

....

The mingling of these three powerful traditions can be seen in the case of a word like *kingly*. The Anglo-Saxons had only one word to express this concept, which, with typical simplicity, they made up from the word king. After the Normans, three synonyms enter the language: *royal, regal*, and *sovereign*.[2]

....

---

[1]Robert McCrum, William Cran, and Robert MacNeil, *The Story of English* (New York: Elisabeth Sifton Books, Viking, 1986), p. 61.
[2]*The Story of English*, p. 75.

As the language developed, the simple, concrete activites of the "people" (who were usually serfs) survived in the large Anglo-Saxon vocabulary that provides the building blocks of the language. The words used for finer, more abstract concepts and distinctions usually find their roots in Latin or sometimes French.

The problem we have in business writing is not whether to use Anglo-Saxon words or the language of the aristocracy. Rather, the issue is how to choose the appropriate word for clear communication and tonal rightness.

Latinate words such as *ameliorate*, *edification*, and *disseminate* have very precise meanings and are used to express fine nuances in a context. Anglo-Saxon words like *kick*, *walk*, and *work* are the vocabulary of common parlance. Times haven't changed so much.

A very special problem with Latinate words arises for business writers. When they use Latinate vocabulary for the purpose of impressing rather than for the purpose of precision, the words are often misused.

Consider these two sentences:

....

1. The following progress report is presented for your *edification*. (Latin root)
2. This progress report will tell you *what has been done*. (Anglo-Saxon)

....

What does the word *edification* mean? According to Webster's it means the "act of instructing or improving, especially in moral and religious knowledge." Thinking back to the use of Latin as the language of the Church, we can understand better its root meaning. *Edification* really has a very narrow meaning. A progress report written in a business situation is unlikely to *edify* anyone.

The point is that oftentimes Latin-based words are actually misused by writers seeking to impress the reader with the sight and sound of an expanded vocabulary. The lack of commonness of these words to most people probably means they don't understand them very clearly when they read them in the first place. And a word like *edification* as used in this sentence actually does miscommunicate because it doesn't mean what the writer thinks it does.

Thus before you use a Latinate word or some other "unfamiliar" word in common parlance, *make sure it means what you think it does*. And given the precision of context necessary for Latinate diction, you'll probably find yourself returning to Anglo-Saxon, everyday language for most business writing. After all, business is mostly concrete actions and activities. Religion, science, literature, and even law are not the stuff of the everyday business world.

However, if your context does require a precise meaning such as that provided by Latinate vocabulary, then by all means use it. And sometimes your context can simply be enriched by the *proper* use of Latinate diction. That is your judgment. As I said earlier, part of developing stylistic flexiblity is the ability to set standards appropriate to the occasion and the reader.

But misuse of a Latinate word obviously will *not* enrich the context or stimulate the reader.

Here is a list of Latin- or Old French-derived words with some simpler equivalents. Ask yourself before using them—do I really need to use this word? Is it precisely what my context calls for?

Why say	*If it's clearer or more correct to say*	
abate	decrease	reduce
accumulate	gather	collect
acquiesce	agree	go along with
additional	added	more
ameliorate	improve	make better
approximately	about	almost
ascertain	find out	make certain
circumvent	avoid	get around
disseminate	distribute	disperse
endeavor	try	attempt
equivalent	equal to	same as
finalize	finish	complete
forfeit	give up	lose
initiate	start	begin
instance	case	example
minimal	least	smallest
numerous	a lot	many
obviate	get around	prevent
optimum	best	foremost
reciprocate	give in return	give back
rectify	correct	improve
require	need	want
rescind	take back	call off
simplistic	simple	easy
solicit	seek	ask for
verify	confirm	check

"Elegant" Phrases

Along with Latinate diction, business writers often use wordy, old-fashioned phrases that mar their writing. As with Latinate diction, they seem to think these phrases make their writing sound more elegant.

Again, there is a historical precedent for this stylistic concept. Since the Renaissance, English writers have revered the classics. They have sought both to embellish their prose with Latinate words and, to some degree, to mirror the syntax of the Latin language. At the same time, a debate emerged in the Renaissance and has been raging ever since over "elegant" writing versus "plain" style.

....

... Shakespeare summarized the debate with a typically striking phrase. When Berowne finally declares his love for Rosaline in *Love's Labour's Lost* he announces that he will shun "taffeta phrases, silken terms precise." Instead

... my wooing mind shall be express'd
In russet yeas and honest kersey noes.[3]

....

Business writers, whether knowingly or unknowingly, have inherited this tradition. How many times have I heard business people in a writing class say, "That sentence flows well" or "That sentence just sounds abrupt to me if you take all those words out."

The desire to "round out" a sentence or to "make it flow" is not bad. This is the elegance English prose stylists have always striven for. You must develop a fine ear, though, to avoid excesses or the mere imitation of a stylistic concept that should be reassessed—first, for its usefulness to a modern business reader, and second, for its very beauty.

I think most of us would agree that Milton's style in "Areopagitica," though elegant and logical, would not communicate in a modern business setting. Of course, it was never intended for

---

[3]*The Story of English,* pp. 95–96.

such a purpose, and few people today would be tempted to use it or even capable of using it.

Many modern business writers, however, still aspire to elegance and a very formal style in their writing. They try to achieve this quality by embellishing their writing with:

a) Latinate vocabulary

b) "Elegant" phrases

Now consider these examples from real business reports which show one or both of these stylistic tendencies.

....

1. Due to the fact that we live in litigious times, it is not seemly for management to act in any way that might promote problematical dealings with respect to potential marketing prospects.

2. We need to formulate an approach to define for us those messages and attitudes optimal for our work environment in order that we may better manage them toward desired results.

3. It is a matter of regret, therefore, that this report on the subject seems so unpromising and that because of this your request for specific recommendations cannot be complied with.

4. If any further information pertaining to this subject is required, do not hesitate to get in touch with me at your convenience.

....

The style of these examples is not really elegant. Certainly, it is not direct and clear.

George Orwell said it best about prose style, I think, in his classic essay, "Politics and the English Language." He lays down five rules of thumb that are just about what I've been saying to you for the last eighty-odd pages. Then he adds, "Break any of these rules sooner than say anything outright barbarous."[4]

Language has rhythm and sound. The rhythms of English, as you've seen, are a blend of many tonalities. Thus you must develop and use your ear. Read your prose aloud. You'll find yourself naturally avoiding awkward phrasing and stylistic ugliness.

Here's a partial list of "elegant" phrases with "plain" equivalents. There are many, many more. They can destroy the "flow" and rhythm of a sentence—and thus, its readability. Good writers train their ears to listen carefully for the intrusive rhythms of these phrases.

Elegant Phrase	*Plain Style*
Acknowledge receipt of	Thank you for your . . .
	I (or we) have received . . .
Along the lines of	like
As per your request	According to (or simply state your reply to the request)
Arrived at the conclusion that	concluded or decided
Due to the fact that	since, because
In accordance with your request	as you asked
Inasmuch as	since
In the amount of	for
In the event that	if
In this connection	(omit the phrase)
Prior to	before
Subsequent to	after
Upon receipt of	When we receive
Until such time as	until
We regret to inform you	We are sorry
With the exception of	except
With reference to	about

---

[4]George Orwell, "Politics and the English Language," reprinted in *A Collection of Essays by George Orwell* (New York: Harcourt Brace Jovanovich, Inc., Harbrace Paperbound Library, 1956), p. 170.

Exercise and Suggested Revisions: Revising "Elegant" Style

Excessive use of Latinate vocabulary and elegant phrasing is not a natural style of speaking or writing in the twentieth century. In Milton's time, people may have spoken like that to some extent, but they don't anymore. And even in Milton's time, the elegance of the style was created to appeal to a certain kind of audience for a certain purpose.

Today, people who write for business in an excessively elegant way had to learn this style of writing. They learned it by imitation and by receiving approval from others who wrote in this way. This style is one type of bureaucratic writing or "officialese" that spreads in some business environments.

Now let's reverse this process of imitation.

First, you'll have the opportunity to read two sentences and change the language. Your goal is to make the style simpler and more direct, the way a twentieth-century business person would be most likely to speak.

After you've revised these two sentences, compare your answers to the suggested revisions. Then you'll revise two more sentences, look at the revisions, two more sentences, and then another two, until you've finally worked through eight revisions. Through this process of revising and checking your revisions, you can become more sensitive to these kinds of problems and develop your ear to hear a simpler, more direct style. *As* we discussed earlier, part of the problem with changing habits of elegant writing is that many people's ears have gotten used to and have even come to approve of the rhythm and vocabulary of this kind of writing.

You may want to refer back to the lists of Latinate words (p. 94) and "elegant" phrases (p. 97) for ideas to use in your revisions. Be sure to revise all the sentences.

Rewrite these sentences. Make them more direct and simplify the language.

....

1. As agreed upon in our meeting of February 28, to assist us in conducting the office equipment inventory, it will be necessary to obtain the services of two "volunteers" on a full-time basis from each department.

Your revision: _____

_____

_____

_____

2. Viewing the program objectively, it could be said that there are various deficiencies which might in future years lead to ramifications such as diminution of earnings.

Your revision: _____

_____

_____

_____

_____

....

Compare your revisions with these. Once again, do not look at the revisions as the "right" answer. Rather, use them as a guide to evaluate your own work. Which do you like better? Why?

....

1. We need two full-time "volunteers" from each department to help us conduct the office equipment inventory.

(Note: If you think it's important to remind the reader of the February 28 meeting, the sentence can begin, "As we agreed on February 28, we need . . .")

2. The program has problems that could lead to reduced earnings.

....

Make these sentences simpler and more direct.

....

3. As you know, the procedure for 1987 will be substantially the same as for 1986, but it will still be necessary to disseminate the procedure to the Personnel Administrators for distribution to the appropriate personnel in their departments.

Your revision: _____

_____

_____

_____

_____

4. Members of the task force are at variance with each other regarding an expeditious solution to the conflict.

Your revision: _____

_____

_____

_____

_____

....

Here are some possible revisions.

....

3. We must send the 1987 version of the procedure to the Personnel Administrators. They should then give their people copies of it.

4. The task force members cannot agree on an easy way to settle the conflict.

....

Make these sentences simpler and more direct.

5. We acknowledge receipt of your letter of recent date advising us of your new address.

Your revision: _____

_____

_____

_____

_____

6. It might be well if the urgency of this situation could be brought to the attention of the departments by means of a memo from us.

Your revision: _____

_____

_____

_____

_____

Here are two possible revisions.

5. We have received your new address.

6. We need to send the departments a memo telling them the problem.

Make these sentences simpler and more direct.

7. I have drafted a possible finalized version of the procedure and it is herewith attached for your perusal.

Your revision: _____

_____

_____

_____

_____

8. The investigation was carried out by the Auditing Department for the purpose of determining the accuracy of the financial statements submitted by us.

Your revision: _____

_____

_____

_____

_____

....

Here are two possible revisions.

....

7. A possible final draft of the procedure is attached for you to read.

8. The Auditing Department has investigated the financial statements we submitted.

....

Is Jargon Good or Bad?

Jargon means *technical language*. It provides a useful medium of communication for people who understand it and is meaningless to everybody else.

Here's an excerpt from a letter by a Marketing Support Analyst working for a major computer company. He's writing to another systems employee:

The Operating System 16.7 will introduce EPFs. This enables runtime code to page into memory directly, bypassing the usage of the paging disk. EPF programs may call other programs (not just subroutines) and will utilize the new BIND utility instead of the SEG-LOADER. Execution time will therefore be greatly enhanced. . . . This revision will also permit the automatic detection of asynchronous baud rate through use of new config directive "ASD."

While this may be "Greek" to most of us, it's perfectly clear to them.

Suppose, however, a physician and patient were to have the following conversation:

Doctor: You have a severe hematoma as a result of your accident. Related stress and anxiety have produced chronic spasms of the duodenum.

Patient: Huh?

Doctor: You have a bad bruise and recurring stomach aches that are probably coming from stress.

Most of us would probably agree that this doctor's bedside manner was lacking. Would most patients know what he's saying? This is an inappropriate use of jargon.

Technicians who use jargon when speaking or writing may do so for good reasons.

- They want to communicate with another technician.
- They want to indicate their membership in a profession, trade, business, or some other sort of specialized fraternity.

In these situations, if you truly "know your stuff," your language signals this to the special group members and you're accepted. If the language is imprecisely used, you're marked and excluded.

When speaking or writing to a layman, however, as in the case of doctor and patient, people's motives for using jargon may be less laudable.

- They want to impress people with their technical status.
- They do not understand their technical world well enough to express it in layman's terms.

Since we live in a world that confers status on people who are professionals or technicians, it's easy to see how anyone might find himself wanting to parade his background. If, however, a technician really commits himself to explaining something technical to a nontechnical reader, he must take the time to define or give examples of terms and concepts unknown to the layman.

In short, the degree to which you should use jargon depends on *whom you're writing for.* An appropriate and good use of jargon is when two scientists, physicians, computer technicians, or other technical specialists are using the language to achieve precision in their communication. Jargon is a kind of shorthand for these people. It would take many words to say what they mean without jargon.

An inappropriate and perhaps even unethical use of jargon is when a contractor of some kind uses the language merely to impress or to sell something to a potential client who really does not understand the language. This is akin to the unethical and manipulative use of abstractions by dictators and demagogues.

When jargon becomes trendy, it often graduates to the status of a *buzzword*. Buzzwords are specious jargon. Their denotative meanings, and thus their technical precision, are lost. Only the glamour of the worlds they came from remains. For example:

Once the departments have *interfaced,* their *outputs* should improve considerably.

These terms, which have technical meanings in the computer world, are vague in this context. But they're still trailing their high-tech aura. Since the writer is apparently talking about improving efficiency, he chose the words more for their suggestive qualities than their meaning.

All disciplines, of course, have their jargon to a greater or lesser extent. Yet jargon, even for the technical reader, can be taken to excess. The degree to which jargon or buzzwords may have permeated your style in a detrimental way is a judgment you must make each time you write. Part of your judgment will hinge on whom you're writing for and what you're writing about. Part will hinge on what your "ear" tells you will be readable.

Here's an example of what one bank vice president's ear told him was an excessive use of jargon:

Company X's asset conversion cycle demands a heavy mix of illiquid assets; further, the industry is subject to definite cyclicality of demand. Having financed its latest growth curve with debt, the company appears to no longer be a viable credit risk. Its ROE makes it an unattractive capital investment, yet its ROS and ALEV are more appropriate to a low value-added operation and its debt-to-worth ratio is more appropriate to a dealer in hedgeable commodities than a captial- and labor-intensive manufacturer in a basic industry. A quick and dirty analysis of its current or working asset quality reveals a working capital inadequacy and an inability to clean up senior liabilities in a high point liquidation even if we were protected by the seniority afforded by a perfected floating lien on all personal assets.

As you've probably realized, I am using *ear* as a metaphor for an aesthetic sense or standard of good writing. I use the term "good writing" to encompass such connotations as *clear, direct, communicative*, and, yes, sometimes even *beautiful*. All good writers are continually developing this inner ear. And if it's really developing, it will be susceptible to change.

To help you become more sensitive to jargon and buzzwords, the chart on page 108 lists some common terms and the specialized worlds they come from. A list of common buzzwords is also provided. Then you'll have the opportunity to revise some sentences that illustrate abuses of these kinds of vocabulary.

Exercise: Jargon and Buzzwords

Revise these sentences so that the message is expressed in simpler, less techical terms. Your tools are:

- eliminating unclear jargon or buzzwords
- adding, changing, deleting, or rearranging parts of the sentence to achieve clarity

1. Management has demonstrated its expertise in the commodity brokerage business and thus the company is viable as a going concern.

2. Competitive pricing structures, the increasing presence of imports, and a projected softening of demand in the industry point to possible profitability problems for the company.

3. I need your feedback regarding devices that will make the deal doable as soon as possible.

4. Our time frame for the project is August 1, 1988, to November 1, 1988.

5. Further improvement of sales is expected as the company focuses on Third World nations which need heavy machinery to build their infrastructure and as the company also continues its emphasis on new product development and the enhancement of sales techniques in its dealer network.

Suggested Revisions: Jargon and Buzzwords

Once again, remember that these are only suggested responses. Yours will undoubtedly be different and may be better.

1. The company is likely to remain in business because skillful commodity brokers manage it.

2. Competitive prices, more imports, and less demand for its products may decrease the company's profits.

3. I need your thoughts about ways to do the deal as soon as possible.

4. The project will begin August 1, 1988, and end by November 1, 1988.

5. The company expects to sell a lot of heavy machinery to developing countries, create new products, and improve the salesmanship of its dealers.

Note: You could keep *Third World* or use *underdeveloped*, although the connotations of these terms have become more and more negative. *Developing* is also economics jargon but carries a more positive connotation.

Legal Jargon	Accounting Jargon	Economics Jargon	Financial Jargon	Computer Jargon	Specious Jargon or Buzzwords
subordinated	balance sheet	infrastructure	tenor	boot up	ultimate
debt	income statement	integration	mitigate	log on	expertise
secured basis	liquidity	a) vertical	spontaneous	bits	implement
attach	liability	b) horizontal	financing	bytes	interface
perfect	factoring	capital-intensive	portfolio	megabytes	impact (verb)
priority	fixed or	labor-intensive	asset protection	data base	transact
guarantee	intangible assets	Third World	seasonality	menu	institute (verb)
lien	plant	diversified	lead bank	command	device
floating lien	credit cycle	cyclicality	run-offs	hard disk	element
personal assets	working capital	elastic	projections	floppy disk	factor
real property	revenue	demand	squeeze	hardware	viable
seniority	expense	underdeveloped	leverage	software	demonstrate
	debit		cushion	window	experience (verb)
	encumbrance		monitor	cursor	enhance
	accounts receivable		bridge financing	memory	prioritize
	accounts payable		profitability	hard drive	logistical
	long-term		going concern	daisy wheel	time frame
	short-term		"attractive client"	printer	responsive
	in the red		lending vehicle	dot matrix	output
	in the black		revolver	printer	input
	expenditure		participation	laser printer	feedback
			classified loan		per
					parameters
					management
					doable
					focus (verb)
					key (adjective)

6

Organization and Logic

Two Ways of Organizing Memorandums

To achieve an appropriate style for a specific business writing occasion, you must adapt your style to speak to the reader in an appropriate way. Similarly, you must consider the reader or group of readers and their needs when you organize the report. This means:

1. Determine what they need or want to know.
2. Arrange that information in a sequence that helps them more readily understand what you have to say. This frequently means stating your main points first and then the reasons that explain those points. This is called "most important to least important" order.*

"Most important to least important" order is preferred by most business readers because it is easy to read. The most important points are clearly stated at the beginning and supporting evidence or arguments are relegated to the body. Busy readers may not choose to read the entire document, but this kind of organization ensures that they will be able to glean your major points easily.

"Most important to least important" order is generally used for:

- summaries
- memorandums
- letters requesting information
- letters replying to requests for information

---

*"Most important to least important" order is sometimes referred to as deductive organization. While this label is accurate in that it implies organizing from general conclusions to specific instances, it is misleading in that most reports organized this way are not based on a pure deductive argument. See pp. 125–130 of this chapter for a fuller consideration of the differences in inductive and deductive logic.

These forms all have one thing in common: the writer must get to the point in the most efficient way possible.

Another pattern of organization commonly used is based on reasoning from specific instances to general conclusions.* In this pattern, the reader is required to follow a trail of logic and analysis laid out by the writer before receiving an important part of the "bottom-line" message, such as a series of specific recommendations, at the end of the report. This kind of pattern, however, still requires an introduction that foreshadows the report's conclusion or gives the reader a structure for understanding how and why the report is organized as it is. Otherwise, the reader will not be motivated to follow the writer's logical trail. This kind of patterning is most often used for:

- research reports
- letters or reports that contain a message the reader will perceive as negative, provocative, controversial, or sensitive
- reports written to a *hostile audience.* In such cases, the writer must explain his reasoning first to enable the reader to understand the bottom-line message and accept an idea that the reader is not sympathetic to.

In short, writers generally organize reports this way when they know they must work through a case slowly and in some detail to gain the reader's acceptance of the message.

Writers tend to encounter the same difficulty, however, in using either of these patterns: *how to begin the report.* Most writers want to tell in the same way that they experienced— usually chronologically or by prolonging presentation of the main points until all the evidence is presented first. Readers,

---

*This kind of organization is often called *inductive* since it is based, in the broadest sense, on inductive logic: reasoning from the particular to the general.

however, find this kind of organization frustrating because they aren't sure of the report's direction. They also have to plow impatiently through more detail than is necessary to understand the writer's message. For example:

The overhead roll-up door at the South Loading Warehouse was 32 feet wide by 20 feet high, in three sections, with sliding vertical structural steel guides separating each of the sections. The center section was 14 feet wide and motor-operated. The side sections were chain-operated. Damage to the sliding vertical guides occurred when they were struck by vehicles using the center opening. This damage caused the side wind locks which run in the vertical guides to fall when buffeted by high winds. The center section along with the vertical guides was so badly damaged that the entire door was made inoperable. Therefore, it was removed by station forces and closed up with wood construction. There is a removable section in this wood closure to accommodate small vehicles. However, when there are large loads to be accommodated, the entire closure must be carefully removed and then reinstalled, taking three hundred man hours to accomplish the work. In the interim while the closure is removed, the interior of the plant is exposed to the weather. The present wood closure which is combustible is subjected to steady deterioration, creating a safety hazard in high winds. Installation of a single heavy-duty motor-operated roll-up door will allow entrance of large trucks without damage to the door. The door can be rapidly closed after trucks have entered, reducing the likelihood of freezing in cold weather.

Although the writer has a good recommendation to make, the reader may not be motivated to stay with the report long enough to gain it. As so often happens, the writer prolonged presentation of the main point until the end. Additionally, he provides no way to help the reader assimilate or understand the mass of detail presented at the beginning.

All writers must capture their readers' attention at the beginning of the document. Two methods of doing this are particularly useful for report writers. One method is writing an opening that *summarizes* the report's message. This kind of opening has long been practiced by newspaper writers and is called the *lead*. Another method is to *whet the readers' appetites* at the beginning so that they will want to read the report to glean the bottom-line message at the end. I call this kind of opening the *hook*.

Summarizing the Story: The Lead

Journalists are always careful to summarize the most significant information *first* in a news story. To ensure a proper news summary, they are trained to answer the questions *who, what, when, where,* and *how* at the beginning. A common news lead might read:

> John K. Smitherson, Chairman of the Advanced Securities Trading Corporation, jumped off the roof of the Highland Motel in downtown Manhattan at 7:00 p.m., October 19, 1987. He was dead on arrival at Bellevue Hospital.

If you want to find out why he jumped, how much money his company lost on Black Monday, how much blood was on the sidewalk, or how many survivors he left, you must read the body of the story to glean the gory details.

The lead is an efficient way of helping the reader quickly grasp the central facts of a story. This method may also be used by report writers, although the content of the lead in business reports will not always be strictly factual. When the report writer summarizes his bottom-line message at the beginning, it can be a conclusion, a recommendation, a decision, or a judgment. The body of the report presents facts, evidence, and logical arguments in support of the main point or points. The report usually ends by the writer asking for any response or follow-up he wants from the readers as a result of their having read the report.

The report on the roll-up door illustrates the most common problem business writers have in writing the lead: *they put at the end what should be at the beginning*. How much clearer that report would have been with an opening such as this:

....

I recommend replacing the door at the South Loading Warehouse with a heavy-duty, motor-operated, roll-up door. The old roll-up door was damaged beyond repair. The opening is now closed with an unsafe temporary wooden structure.

....

This revision also illustrates that a good lead is not always achieved by making sure you don't have at the end what really belongs in the beginning. Important information was also scattered throughout the body that needed to be included in the lead.

Look at these excerpts from a report in which the lead elements were widely scattered throughout the body of the report:

....

First sentence: "The following is a summary of the positions we took regarding a request to IRS for a change in accounting."

Paragraph 2: "*Unbilled revenues*: [details]. . .No change in accounting was deemed necessary." [conclusion]

Paragraph 3: "*Bi-monthly pilot project*: [details] . . . A change in accounting is not necessary." [conclusion]

Paragraph 4: *"Budget billing:* [details] . . . We requested a change in accounting." [conclusion]

Paragraph 5: *"New York State Sales Tax:* [details] . . . We did not request a change in accounting." [conclusion]

Lead rewrite: Here is a summary of why we asked IRS for a change in accounting for budget billing and did not request a change for unbilled revenues, the bi-monthly pilot project, or New York State Sales Tax. [Lead summarizes the report's four major conclusions.]

....

Sometimes a good lead can be a single sentence. For example:

....

"We had no major problems this month."

....

This lead is from a monthly progress report on system installation problems. From this, the writer's boss could have assumed that what followed concerned minor problems, and, in fact, might have stopped reading after the first sentence.

Before you can write the lead for your own reports, you will have to decide what main points you want to make. While this may sound obvious and easy, anyone who has ever done any writing knows that this is probably the most difficult part of writing. Sometimes you don't know what your main points are until you've tried to write a draft. That's why the main points so often do not emerge until the end of the first draft. Part of the redrafting process then involves pulling them up to the beginning.

One good way to practice writing leads is to write them for other writers' disorganized reports that either bury the message at the end or scatter it piecemeal throughout the report.

This is good training to help you tighten up your own drafts by checking for the most common spots of organizational weakness. With practice, you'll overcome the natural tendency to narrate all your findings first and will become more deft at "starting with the bottom line."

Now you'll have the opportunity to write an improved lead for someone else's report. After that, we'll move to the second technique I mentioned: the hook.

Exercise: The Lead

The following is a typical report that could profit from a lead that summarizes its main points. In the space provided, draft a lead that makes the report's purpose clearer. Remember to search for important points that have been either buried at the end or scattered piecemeal throughout the report.

....

TO: Divisions A to Z

FROM: John Jones, V.P.

SUBJECT: *Items in Short Supply*

We are all aware of the energy crisis and the steps being taken by the company to promote its prudent handling. However, less well known are several other items and commodities currently in short supply nationally and projected to remain in short supply for months to come. They include:

1. *Paper and paper-related items*—Supply very tight, and conservatively projected to remain so this year. Many items on allocation by the mills.
2. *Lumber*—Supply tight, especially pine and hardwood items.
3. *Cotton rags*—Scarce and becoming more so due to replacement of cotton by synthetic textiles.
4. *Steel*—Currently on allocation by the mills, with this year's production projected at 5% less than last year's production.
5. *Copper*—Currently on mill allocation, with deliveries growing more uncertain.

6. *Paint*—Petrochemical resins and solvents not available as essential paint ingredients, due to concentration of petroleum industry on fuel production.

Traditionally, these items have been so readily available that conservation and restraint were not required. This is no longer the case. The Purchasing Department is making every effort to assure a continued supply. However, it is increasingly important that discipline and planning be employed in their use. The purpose of this memorandum is to highlight these facts and to solicit your attention and assistance.

Your lead:_____

_____

_____

_____

_____

Suggested Revisions: The Lead

Compare your lead with these suggested revisions. Notice that both of them took most of their content from the *end* of the report. The language has also been made simpler and the sentences are more direct.

Revision 1: "We ask your help in conserving the commodities listed below so that the Purchasing Department can continue to supply them. They are in short supply nationwide and will remain so for months."

Revision 2: "We must start to be very conservative in using the following items. They are in short supply nationally and will probably remain scarce for months."

Whetting the Reader's Appetite: The Hook

When writers put the bottom-line message at the end of the report, they must invite readers to enter into their thinking process or follow trails of evidence with them. This kind of writing requires involvement from readers. Involvement implies motivation. Readers need encouragement and other kinds of stimulation to motivate them to follow the writer's path.

Thus when you use this kind of organization, you must "hook" your readers into wanting to read the report. Otherwise, they are likely either not to read it or to skim it superficially. And if you take the trouble to lay out your case before stating an important conclusion or recommendation, you've done so because you want your readers to follow your arguments *carefully*.

Novelists are perhaps the most skilled of all writers at hooking readers. Since a novel may range from a hundred to a thousand pages, readers must be enticed immediately to commit themselves. Usually novelists don't want to give away the story at the beginning, so summarizing the plot is rarely a favored strategy. How, then, do novelists manage to engage their readers in journeys of such epic scope?

Let's take a moment to look at the opening of one of the most successful and famous novels in English: *Tarzan of the Apes* by Edgar Rice Burroughs.

....

I heard this story from one who had no business to tell it to me, or to any other. I may credit the seductive influence of an old vintage upon the narrator for the beginning of it, and my own skeptical incredulity during the days that followed for the balance of the strange tale.[1]

....

---

[1]Edgar Rice Burroughs, *Tarzan of the Apes* (New York: Ballantine Books, January 1976), p. 1.

From the opening sentence, the writer engages the reader by promising a tale so strange and bizarre that only the "seductive influence of an old vintage" could have wrung it from the narrator. Through a few carefully chosen descriptive phrases—"one who had no business to tell it," "seductive influence," "my own skeptical incredulity," and "strange tale"—Burroughs piques the reader's interest. The novelist then proceeds to spin out the tale at his chosen pace.

Similarly, the descriptive power of language coupled with an attempt to involve the reader can transform a pedestrian report opening into one that whets the reader's appetite. For example, look at the opening of a report detailing a number of discrepancies found in an audit the writer reviewed. The report ended with recommendations for establishing a departmental review with auditors before allowing publication of audit reports.

....

Original Opening: I reviewed this audit and found a number of discrepancies. We should review reports with our auditors before publication.

....

It does the job but it's not involving. Now look at a revised version the author came up with.

....

When you read how many discrepancies I found when I reviewed this audit, I think you'll agree we should review audit reports with our auditors before publication.

....

The difference comes from one descriptive phrase, "how many," and from taking the time to challenge the readers to find out for themselves if what the writer says is true. If readers are involved, they are more likely to read a report thoughtfully. In a case like this, where acceptance of the recommendations at the end hinges on the readers' concurring in the writer's conclusion, it's essential that they be motivated to read the case thoroughly.

Like novelists, you must exercise your creativity to hook your readers. That means thinking about what would be likely to involve them in reading your case. Burroughs knew enough about human psychology to realize that people love an exotic tale, especially if it carries the promise of adventure or danger. While this technique may not often be available to report writers, there are some standard opening techniques that have been used equally well by creative writers and business writers. They are:

- Pique the reader's curiosity by posing questions that will be answered in the report.
- Foreshadow the report's findings or conclusions. For example:

....

  - "You will be able to see that _____ ."
  - "You will be a able to see the effect that _____ has on _____ ."
  - "You will be able to understand the impact of _____ (some unusual occurrence)."

....

- Engage the reader in an exploration. For example:

....

  - "I've given some thought to _____ ."

- "I'd like to describe _____ ."

....

- Challenge the reader. For example:

....

  - "You will be surprised to find out _____ ."
  - "You would normally expect to see _____ in these circum-stances, but this report will show that _____ (some unex-pected results occurred)."
  - "This study will show that while _____ might be expected, _____ actually occurred."

....

One might say that, in the broadest sense, Burroughs' tech-nique is simply a variation on "engaging the reader in an ex-ploration." Whether you're a creative writer or a business writer, you'll have to reach your readers psychologically as well as intellectually if you're going to "hook" them.

Exercise: Recognizing Effective Hooks

Here are seven examples of the openings of business reports in which the writers attempted to hook their readers. As you read them, be aware of their effect on you as a reader. How likely would you be to want to read the report, based on the opening sentences? Note your response to each example with a "yes" or "no." Then in the space labeled "Why?" explain what appealed to you or what put you off.

....

1. To determine the best way to teach writing skills to our employ-ees, I conducted a study that asked three questions:

- Do these people need training?
- If so, what kind do they need?

- How can we better manage the development of people's writing skills on an ongoing basis once the training class is over?

I will present my findings and answers to these questions in this report.

Your response: _____

Why? _____

2. A centralized purchasing system has been established whereby Appleby Company can improve the securing of essential materials. This system, once it becomes fully operational, will help us achieve our primary goal of attaining raw materials when needed along with additional auxiliary benefits. This is not presently operational due to the following.

Your response: _____

Why? _____

3. At the request of John K. Smitherson, I am documenting my conclusions about the problems currently existing with our management development curriculum.

Your response: _____

Why? _____

4. Your collective response to the questionnaire we recently sent out was unanimous: we must recruit a very special kind of person to lead this department.

Your response: _____

Why? _____

5. "People learn by doing" is the principle I followed in designing the attached teaching plan.

Your response: _____

Why? _____

6. The majority of data required for the first phase of conversion has been received and entered into the data bases. The progress of the system has been affected by the trauma of data collection but significant progress continues to be made. During our first efforts at departmental allocations of time-sharing expenditures, a number of observations were made. Some of these have resulted in the following changes designed both to facilitate the feedback process and to provide better information to you.

Your response: _____

Why? _____

7. Have you ever logged on to your terminal or PC expecting to see your main menu but instead find the message "Reconnected"? Or maybe you hit the enter key and got no response at all?

Your response: _____

Why? _____

Commentary: Recognizing Effective Hooks

Most readers polled about these examples have found 1, 4, 5, and 7 more appealing than 2, 3, and 6. The reasons they gave were:

1. Posing questions aroused curiosity and gave readers a sense of the scope and organizational plan of the report.

2. Although the strategy of suggesting a benefit to the new system was potentially appealing, the language was so technical and the sentence structure so turgid that the strategic strength was lost.

3. The phrase "documenting my conclusions" suggested to most readers something that should be buried in a musty file.

4. The phrase "very special kind of person," though not specific, piqued most people's interest to read on to gain a clearer picture of such a person, especially since their own responses held the key to defining this phrase.

5. The technique of foreshadowing the content of the teaching plan aroused readers' curiosity.

6. Responses were similar to those given for example 2. The language and sentence structure prevented readers from understanding the message and, therefore, from caring about the value the changes may have had for them.

7. Most readers polled said the questions were effective because they spoke directly to the report's readers about their problems.

Inductive versus Deductive Logic

No book on writing is complete without looking at the subject of logic, for logic is the foundation of organization. You already know a lot more about it than you may realize.

Logic is defined by one authority as "the study of the strength of the evidential link between the premises and conclusions of arguments."[2] Academic logicians, of whom Aristotle was perhaps the most influential, fashion these links with relentless in-

---

[2]Brian Skyrms, *Choice and Chance: An Introduction to Inductive Logic*, Third Edition (Belmont, California: Wadsworth Publishing Company, 1986), p. 4.

tellectual precision. In everyday business life, one must also take care that the evidence and reasoning underlying decisions are strong and valid. If decisions are not reasonable given the facts of a situation, the actions taken on the basis of them are not likely to yield useful or profitable results.

Since logic is such a precise subject, there are many misconceptions about it. One of the most common is what makes an argument deductive or inductive.

....

One of the most widespread misconceptions of logic is the belief that deductive arguments proceed from the general to the specific, and inductive arguments proceed from the specific to the general. Such a view is nonsense, for . . . arguments do not fall into two categories: deductive and inductive. . . . the difference between inductively strong and deductively valid arguments is not to be found in the generality or particularity of premises and conclusion but rather in the definitions of deductive validity and inductive strength.[3]

....

If you're tearing your hair out by now, I'm not surprised. But there are a couple of important points suggested here about induction and deduction that are useful for everyday business thinkers and writers to consider. First, the "widespread misconception" the writer refers to has nevertheless been of some use in helping people think about organizing their thoughts on paper. (Thus you'll see many textbooks refer to the two ways of organizing reports that we discussed earlier as "deductive" and "inductive" organization.) But the really important point here is that the true strength of any argument lies in *how valid it really is.* Validity comes from the truth of the evidence pre-

---

[3]Skyrms, pp. 13, 15.

sented and the reasonableness of the links between evidence and conclusions.

The mark of a true deductive argument is that the conclusion *must* be true if the premises are true. The classic deductive argument is the syllogism:

All men are mortal.
Aristotle is a man.
Therefore, Aristotle is mortal.

Syllogisms embody the same reasoning process you followed when you did proofs in geometry class. Geometric proofs start with a principle or axiom whose truth is absolute. You reason from this axiom through a series of interlocking steps, each of which necessarily follows from the previous step. If your logic is sound and you've not skipped a step, your conclusion is proved and must be valid. Milton used a deductive chain of reasoning in the excerpt you saw earlier from "Areopagitica,"[4] basing his argument on beliefs that would have been considered "axiomatic" in his time.

Inductive logic is more creative than deductive logic. In an inductive argument, the conclusion goes beyond the factual claims of the premises. For example:

• Four women carrying bouquets and wearing long dresses were seen entering the church.

---

[4]See Chapter 1, p. 8.

- Four men wearing tuxedos and boutonnieres were seen entering the church.
- The minister was seen entering the church.

Therefore, it is likely that a wedding is about to take place in the church.

....

As our logical authority puts it, "an inductively strong argument risks more than a deductively valid one; it risks the possibility of leading from true premises to a false conclusion."[5] In this example, all the people observed might have been attending a ball being held in the church, though this conclusion does not seem as probable as the other conclusion.

The endpoint of an inductive argument is the discovery of a new fact or insight. The ability to create a theory or conceptualize a really new idea is a creative act of induction. Scientists, conceptualizers, and philosophers pray for this moment to happen to them as they pursue their research or study in their particular discipline. Yet no one really knows where this marvelous ability comes from. For example, we've heard of great theories appearing to scientists in dreams or in other seemingly "illogical" ways.

Happily, we all have this wonderful ability to a greater or lesser extent. It's the same thing that happens when, after studying a difficult subject for a long time, you finally understand a concept or grasp the meaning of something.

Business writing, like all other writing, is only as good as the thinking that underlies it. And business people, like scientists, logicians, or anyone who purports to reach conclusions on the basis of a logical process, will intuitively and naturally use in-

---
[5]Skyrms, p. 8.

ductive and deductive logic. Their writing will contain statements of the "insights" or conclusions they present, supported by a logical way of proving the validity or, at least, acceptability of those insights.

Given the nature of these two reasoning processes and their conclusions, you'll find that most everyday arguments, if analyzed, are inductive rather than deductive. Most real-life situations cannot be made to conform easily to the rigors of deductive logic. As you can imagine, arguments presented in strict syllogistic form, though airtight, are necessarily repetitious and sometimes pedantic. A paragraph might lend itself to this pattern more easily than a whole report, and it is at the level of presenting evidence that you'll sometimes see a true deductive argument. Since inductive arguments allow the writer a greater measure of creativity and opportunities for discovery, the overall logic of a report is usually inductive.

If we think of the organization of business writing in terms of a continuum, then we'd have to say that the two extremes of organization are pure deductive argumentation and merely stating an opinion without any supporting evidence. Business writing will generally fall somewhere between these two extremes.

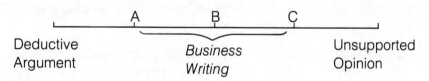

| | A | B | C | |
| Deductive
Argument | | *Business*
Writing | | Unsupported
Opinion |

You as a writer must choose your point on this continuum for each and every communication.

For example, if you place yourself at point C, near the extreme of unsupported opinion, you'll probably choose a method of organization such as "most important to least important order." That is, you will probably state your opinion, decision, conclusion, or recommendation first, and then the reasoning supporting your position. That reasoning could be inductive, deductive, or a combination of the two, but the emphasis of the report is clearly on *your position*.

If you wish to be at point A, your emphasis will be on organizing a logical journey for the readers in order to help them enter into your thinking process so that they will be more likely to agree with your position. The report emphasizes the *importance of your logical process* as much as the conclusion or result of your logic. You're inviting readers to enter your thinking and judge the results of it independently. Again, your logic could be deductive, inductive, or a combination of the two.

If you wish to be at point B on the continuum, then you'd probably use a logical journey as a basic organizing strategy, but maybe you'd take more shortcuts and require more intellectual leaps from your readers in following your logic than you did at point A. By providing them a less-detailed roadmap of your thinking, you'd be assuming that they need less explanation, persuading, or "hand-holding" to understand you than your readers at point A.

Once again, it's thinking about the readers and determining what *they need or want to know* that forms the basis of your plan of organization. There are as many points on this continuum as there are different kinds of readers.

Next, you'll read some business reports that argue inductively. Three types of possible readers are described for each report. Decide which reader would find the report most persuasive and note *why* you think so.

Exercise: Logic and Argumentation

You're going to have the opportunity to read three business reports that attempt to persuade through logical argument.

You'll then be asked to decide which of the following readers would find the report most persuasive.

....

1. A reader who already has knowledge of the case being presented and is especially interested in *your position*. On our continuum of report organization, this is the reader at point C—the one nearest the extreme of "unsupported opinion."

2. A reader who has very little knowledge of the case being presented and who needs a thorough explanation of facts and reasoning to be persuaded. On our continuum, this is the reader near point A—the one who needs to be invited to enter your thinking process in order to be persuaded of your conclusions.

3. A reader who may have some knowledge of the case being presented, but who will still require considerable explanation to be persuaded. This is the reader near point B on our continuum—the one with whom you might take more logical shortcuts than the reader at point A.

....

Here's the continuum. Refer back to pages 129–130 for explanations of its points if you need to.

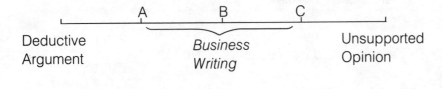

A	B	C
Deductive Argument	*Business Writing*	Unsupported Opinion

....

Report Example Number One

Subject: *Progress Report on Centralized Purchasing*

As you are aware, a letter was released from this office regarding our new corporate policy of reporting all purchase contracts in excess of ten thousand dollars. To date, we have received no response from the manufacturing facilities. There are a number of possible explanations for this with varying implications.

First, it is possible that $10,000 was an inappropriate level in that most contracts negotiated were under this level. An appropriate response to this problem would be to reassess historic purchasing levels in order to establish an appropriate threshold.

Second, the problem may have resulted from the fact that the letter was released on a date too close to the peak buying season, thus not allowing the respective executives adequate time to assimilate the request into their current purchasing procedures. Should this be the case, we should begin to realize the expected benefits of the new directive when the next buying cycle begins.

Third, the problem may represent a message from the purchasing executives that they resent head office tampering with their established routines. In this event, we would need to make them realize the benefits that everyone will gain if they comply with this procedure.

In my opinion, the first explanation is most likely. An appropriate course of action at this point would be to arrange a conference of all the purchasing executives to discuss the problem as a group. Such a conference would also allow us to talk to each executive.

....

This memo would be most persuasive to:

Reader 1, at point C on the continuum _____ .
Reader 2, at point A on the continuum _____ .
Reader 3, at point B on the continuum _____ .

Why?_____

_____

_____

_____

_____

....

Report Example Number Two

Subject: *Approval of $3MM Line of Credit to Russ Yelverton, Inc.*

Introduction: The requested line would be used to purchase putty and cleaning solvents to give the company twelve months' worth of supplies. Volume discounts are important to Yelverton's cost control and will continue its competitive advantage. The low-budget car-painting business is subject to increasing competition. Yelverton is protecting its market share through cost-effective measures such as volume discounts.

Credit Considerations: Yelverton's conservative balance sheet and low-interest expense point to a large debt capacity. Leverage ratios are low since the company has very little debt. Debt is supported by high owner's equity of 69.6%.

Management is protecting its market niche with cost controls and expansion into new markets. Management has plans to add 25 shops in the United States this year and has already opened three new shops in London. Industry trends are favorable because consumers are keeping old cars longer. As the market leader and founder of the quick and easy paint job, Yelverton is dedicated to its primary business.

Cost controls and expanded markets mark Yelverton's corporate philosophy. Cost of goods sold to sales was up to 88.5% in 1986 from 85.2% in 1985. The purchase of volume discounts will help Yelverton cut costs and thus preserve its market niche of "no frills paint jobs."

Recommendation: Approval of the $3MM line is requested.

....

This memo would be most persuasive to:

Reader 1, at point C on the continuum _____ .
Reader 2, at point A on the continuum _____ .
Reader 3, at point B on the continuum _____ .

Why?_____

_____

_____

_____

_____

_____

Report Example Number Three

Subject: *Findings of Program Evaluation*

I have just completed the first part of the evaluation you requested that I do of our Financial Analysis Preparatory Program. So that I could evaluate the quality of our courses from the student's standpoint, I took three courses our department has been offering for several years: Capital Markets, International Finance, and Corporate Finance. I also took and passed all the exams. The courses, however, were not a totally productive learning experience because their learning objectives were far too broad and ambitious in scope given (1) the entering knowledge of the average learner and (2) the time allotted for each course.

You may be surprised to find out that these courses are each only two days long yet purport to teach recent historical developments, the most important theoretical developments, and a fairly generous sampling of some important technical tools common to each subject. The average student is a recent college graduate with a B.A. in business or a general liberal arts degree. The material was new to most of them. As a result, they focused their attention on taking copious notes and "cramming" for the final exam. After the exam, the information was promptly forgotten—at least, that was my experience and the experience of twenty other students I spoke to.

For these courses to result in successful retention of learning, they should be redesigned and, in my opinion, should also be made much more narrow in scope. We cannot hope to provide students with either a broad or a deep acquaintance with these subjects in a few days. And the question is—do we even want to try? For example, some things must be memorized, but some can be looked up when needed. One may need to know only where and how to locate the information. As the courses are currently taught, however, we require memorization of a wide range of assorted facts and principles, most of which bear little relevance to anything the student will immediately do.

If a proper assessment of the needs inherent in these courses were done, it would then be possible for our staff to design the curriculum and teaching strategies that would really meet those needs. I believe a professional instructional designer could help us clarify our needs so that we would be able to produce more relevant and successful courses than the ones I attended. Since our boss has been talking about upgrading these courses for a long time, this seems like the right time to give her an action plan to start the ball rolling. Could we set a date sometime next week to put together a full set of recommendations? I'd also like to discuss some other reactions I had to the courses I took.

....

This memo would be most persuasive to:

Reader 1, at point C on the continuum _____ .
Reader 2, at point A on the continuum _____ .
Reader 3, at point B on the continuum _____ .

Why?_____

_____

_____

_____

_____

Commentary: Logic and Argumentation

1. Report example number one would probably be most persuasive to reader number 1, the reader near point C who is primarily interested in the writer's position. Although the writer presents some indication of his reasoning process, the evidence that caused him to prefer one of the positions he presents over the others is not stated. Thus the final conclusion of the report is little more than an unsupported opinion.

   This kind of strategy is risky at best. Probably only a couple of sentences would be needed to explain the opinion stated in the last paragraph. Unless the reader is the writer's good buddy, he or she is likely to feel annoyed by the omission of any explanation for the final conclusion.

2. Report example number two would probably be most persuasive to reader number 3, the reader near point B on the continuum. The writer presents some evidence and reasoning for the decision, but the argument rests to a large degree on thinly supported assertions. Here are some examples:

   ....

   A. "The low-budget-car paint business is subject to increasing competition. Yelverton is protecting its market share through cost-effective measures such as volume discounts."

   Comment on logic: What's the relationship between cutting costs and staving off the competition?

B. "As the market leader and founder of the quick and easy paint job, Yelverton is dedicated to its primary business."

Comment on logic: Even though a company has invented a product and is the leading seller of the product, these facts alone do not ensure that the company will continue to dedicate itself to producing and selling this product as its primary business. Indeed, the whole paragraph that this sentence comes from has no logic unless the reader already knows a lot more about the company and its strategies than the writing presents.

C. "The purchase of volume discounts will help Yelverton cut costs and thus preserve its market niche of 'no frills paint jobs.' "

Comment on logic: This is the same assertion we discussed in point A: how will cutting costs help stave off the competition and preserve the company's market niche? The report makes this point over and over again (talk about belaboring!) but never explains the reasoning behind the conclusion.

The writer assumes the reader knows that in the low-cost car-painting industry, the market leader has traditionally been the vendor who can offer the lowest prices. One way to keep prices down is to keep costs down. Thus any cost savings resulting from this purchase can be passed along to the customers.

If the reader is well acquainted with this company, its competition, and the industry in which it operates, he or she can color in a lot of the evidential links that are missing from this report. For anyone else, the report is little more than a loosely assembled string of unsupported assertions, some of which are repeated several different ways in lieu of real evidence. In some ways, this report is closer to the realm of unsupported opinion than the first example, though the report emphasizes argumentation over the writer's opinion.

3. Report example number three would probably be most persuasive to reader number 2, the reader near point A on the continuum. The report works through considerable explanation and evidence before presenting its final recommendation that they should hire an instructional designer.

The ending also indicates that the writer probably had a lot of other arguments and evidence to present in support of her case, but elected to present only the main one in the report. This is a good strategy if your readers, like many busy professionals, prefer to read reports that are as short as possible. Some executives refuse ever to read more than a one-page report. Thus sometimes a report must serve as the hook for a fuller discussion of the case in some other forum.

7

Explaining the Main Points

The Paragraph

Paragraphs are the building blocks business writers use to build the report's structure. Reports, like buildings, can be solid edifices only if the overall plan is architecturally sound, the blocks themselves are well made, and the mortar that holds them together is firm.

A report is like a well-made building in that the sequence of the paragraphs reflects the author's logic, the transitions help the reader follow the logic the argument is built on, and the paragraphs themselves explain the main points of the argument. Let's look now at reports from the smallest structural component outward: *Paragraph Development*, *Paragraph Sequencing*, and *Transitions*.

Paragraph Development

Once you've hooked your readers' interest or summarized your main points in the lead, you've got to decide how to explain your thinking in the rest of the report. Clearly, the first paragraph cannot tell the whole story. The body of the report must supply the details and arguments the readers need to comprehend your thinking fully.

You'll recall we spoke earlier about a couple of thought processes that yield ways of organizing paragraphs. Let me refresh your memory:

Cause and effect analysis means explaining why an event had a certain result or how a certain result stemmed from a particular event.

Comparison and contrast means comparing a group of similarities, a group of differences, or a combination of the two in explaining a general point.

Now I'll add a definition of a third process:

Giving examples is the way you *illustrate* a general point with concrete examples.

These ways of organizing arise easily and nonmechanically as you think and write. No one consciously says to himself, "I am now going to organize this paragraph by using comparison and contrast." Rather, as someone explains what he thinks— say, in the case of approving a customer's request for a personal loan—he may decide to point out that the customer has $10,000 more in her savings account in 1988 than she did in 1987. He naturally *contrasts* these two figures to show that the customer's savings have increased. Then from there he might want to go further, based on the evidence, to argue that the customer's increased savings indicate an improvement in her overall financial position *because* of something else the banker knows about her. Now he's using cause and effect analysis. And, of course, the original example of $10,000 is an illustration as well as a comparison.

Cause and effect analysis involves questioning the *reasons* that something happened and is often used in problem solving. If you ask the question, "Why did this happen?" your answer will be the causes. If your question is, "What will this result in?" your answer will be the effects. When you say, "The company is losing money because of poor cost controls, high salaries, and incompetent management," you are dealing with cause. When you say, "The company's poor cost controls, high salaries, and incompetent management will probably make it go bankrupt," you are dealing with effect. Cause explains the past while effect predicts the future.

Comparison means analyzing the ways in which two things are alike, while contrast is analyzing the ways they are unlike. As a developmental technique, comparisons or contrasts can be isolated examples in a paragraph or large-scale organizing strategies.

The first and most important step of any comparison or contrast is deciding on the points to be compared or contrasted. For example, let's say you want to develop the idea that a good manager of people can easily be distinguished from a bad manager of people. To do this, you would ask yourself in what areas you want to contrast the activities of bad managers with good managers. Let's say you choose three points of contrast: (1) time spent on counseling, (2) division of workload, (3) willingness to praise. A simple and useful outline would be three parallel columns like this:

	Good Managers	*Bad Managers*
1. Time spent on counseling	Manager keeps an open-door policy and encourages dialogue with subordinates.	Manager is inaccessible or tends to hide in his office. Questions are ignored or evaded.
2. Division of workload	Manager divides workload fairly among subordinates and according to their talents.	Manager shows favoritism, giving the best assignments to personal favorites.
3. Willingness to praise	Manager gives frequent encouragement and suggests ways to improve.	Manager never gives a compliment but is quick to criticize.

After you've done your outline, you turn it into prose by adding the transitional words and phrases that will help the reader follow the points of the contrast. The transitional words and sentences are italicized.

After working in an office for a while, most people can easily distinguish a good manager of people from a bad manager of people. One immediately noticeable characteristic of good managers is their "open-door" policy. Employees know they can, in most cases, drop by without an appointment to discuss a problem or ask a question. Bad managers, *on the other hand,* shy away from dialogue and hide in their offices with the door closed. Even making an appointment does not ensure a conference, for the employee is often bumped for "more important meetings" or sudden changes in the boss's schedule.

Another clearcut difference between good and bad managers is the way they assign work. The good manager gives considerable thought to employees' skills, talents, and interests before giving out projects. Sometimes a task that will be difficult is assigned to develop an employee's area of weakness, but the major criterion is always which employee can do do the job most successfully. Bad managers, *however*, tend to give the plum assignments to their favorites, even if someone else could do them better. Work is therefore divided politically, according to the managers' personal likes and dislikes. They rarely consider who would be the best person for the job.

Good and bad managers differ markedly in their willingness to give a compliment. Good managers are glad to give credit where credit is due, and often praise good work. When they see an area in which an employee can improve, they offer specific but sensitive suggestions. *On the contrary*, bad managers are quick to criticize, but rarely, if ever, give compliments. In fact, personal comments to employees of any kind are terse and few.

When analyzing through comparison or contrast, keep in mind that you must give equal attention to *both* sides. Otherwise, your analysis will be slanted and one-sided.

Illustration of points is one of the simplest and most natural ways writers explain themselves. A good example is often remembered long after the point it illustrated is forgotten. Examples also often capture attention and interest the reader in hearing a point before it is actually stated.

....

Recently, I met a commercial banker in his fifties who told me the following: "You know, not too long ago all that a commercial banker had to do to generate business was to handle a knife and fork and play golf." That was in the era when banks were regulated and competitors were few. Today, bankers play an entirely different game.

....

The example quoted at the beginning is striking, a little funny, and likely to "hook" the reader into the paragraph. Examples provide detail, color, and liveliness in writing. Without them, the reader is never really sure of exactly what the writer thinks, for the writing lacks specificity. A writer should not expect the reader to color in the examples illustrating his points.

Writers need to be able to recognize the ways these thought processes manifest themselves in writing, not so that they will select any one in particular but so that they can select *them all* and naturally weave them together.

One way to become clearer about how to let these processes happen is to recognize when they have been used by other people in their writing. You'll now have the opportunity to identify these thought processes "in action."

Exercise: Paragraph Development

Read the following paragraphs. You'll notice that certain sections of sentences have been numbered. In the spaces provided after each paragraph, which are numbered to correlate with the italicized parts of the paragraph, identify whether the italicized section shows a use of cause and effect analysis, comparison, contrast, or illustration.

Paragraph Number One

We have known for some time that (1) *since the profit economics of commercial banking have changed, traditional credit products are no longer sufficient* to meet the wide range of credit and noncredit financing options available to the largest corporations. Hence, (2) *the predominant lending focus of the commercial banker has given way* to a more broad-based financial marketing role. (3) *Metro Bank, through the unique strengths of its relationship marketing and management approach, may have a competitive advantage* in the race among banks to reposition themselves in the marketplace.

Example 1: _____
Example 2: _____
Example 3: _____

Paragraph Number Two

Effective January 1, 1987, the Tax Reform Act of 1986 will alter the tax treatment of meals and entertainment expenses. (1) *Under the prior law, these expenses were 100% deductible* when proved to be directly related to the active conduct of Bufoe Corporation's business. (2) *However, under the Tax Reform Act of 1986, business-related meal and entertainment expenses are only 80% deductible* with some exceptions.

Example 1: _____
Example 2: _____

Paragraph Number Three

At present, no standard of taste has been endorsed by management for the Executive Summary's organization. In fact, the general policy has been to encourage employees to avoid using a model for the summary and instead to exercise "creativity" in constructing their format. At the same time, however, (1) *some managers have informally circulated a memo dated May 1, 1987, for employees to use as a model.* Since each case is unique, the same format will not apply to every report. (2) *Thus when employees attempt to apply the model format to their writing, they usually have problems.*

Example 1: _____
Example 2: _____

Paragraph Number Four

Cranford Corporation continued to repay long-term debt and short-term borrowings. (1) *Trade payables increased slightly in line with receivables.* Liquidity was generally maintained. (2) *Cash flow from earnings, conversion of debentures into equity, and a reduction in working investment have enabled Cranford Corporation to reduce leverage to the lowest level of any of the major trading companies.* Subsidiaries are also generally well capitalized, and (3) *the consolidated statements show an even stronger balance sheet than the statements of the individual subsidiaries.* The company has good banking relationships, (4) *especially with Jumbo Bank and The National Trust Company.*

Example 1: _____
Example 2: _____
Example 3: _____
Example 4: _____

Commentary: Paragraph Development

Compare your responses with these. You may have gotten some different answers in a few cases. Example 3 in Paragraph Number Four is both an illustration and a contrast. Example 1 in Paragraph Number Two is both an example and a part of the larger strategy of contrast underlying the paragraph. Not all examples of thought processes can be *absolutely* classified as one thing or another. It's important to try to classify these processes only so that *you can become more conscious of your natural ability to use them* in your thinking and, as a result, in your writing.

....

Paragraph Number One

We have known for some time that (1) *since the profit economics of commercial banking have changed, traditional credit products are no longer sufficient* to meet the wide range of credit and noncredit financing options available to the largest corporations. Hence, (2) *the predominant lending focus of the commercial banker has given way* to a more broad-based financial marketing role. (3) *Metro Bank, through the unique strengths of its relationship marketing and management approach, may have a competitive advantage* in the race among banks to reposition themselves in the marketplace.

Example 1: cause and effect analysis
Example 2: cause and effect analysis
Example 3: cause and effect analysis

....

Paragraph Number Two

Effective January 1, 1987, the Tax Reform Act of 1986 will alter the tax treatment of meals and entertainment expenses. (1) *Under the prior law, these expenses were 100% deductible* when proved to be directly related to the active conduct of Bufoe Corporation's business. (2) *However, under the Tax Reform Act of 1986, business-related meal and entertainment expenses are only 80% deductible* with some exceptions.

Example 1: illustration
Example 2: contrast

....

Paragraph Number Three

At present, no standard of taste has been endorsed by management for the Executive Summary's organization. In fact, the general policy has been to encourage employees to avoid using a model for the summary and instead to exercise "creativity" in constructing their format. At the same time, however, (1) *some managers have informally circulated a memo dated May 1, 1987,* for employees to use as a model. Since each case is unique, the same format will not apply to every report. (2) *Thus when employees attempt to apply the model format to their writing, they usually have problems.*

Example 1: illustration
Example 2: cause and effect analysis

....

Paragraph Number Four

Cranford Corporation continued to repay long-term debt and short-term borrowings. (1) *Trade payables increased slightly in line with receivables.* Liquidity was generally maintained. (2) *Cash flow from earnings, conversion of debentures into equity, and a reduction in working investment have enabled Cranford Corporation to reduce leverage to the lowest level of any of the major trading companies.* Subsidiaries are also generally well capitalized, and (3) *the consolidated state-*

*ments show an even stronger balance sheet than the state-
ments of the individual subsidiaries.* The company has good
banking relationships, (4) *especially with Jumbo Bank and
The National Trust Company.*

Example 1: illustration
Example 2: cause and effect analysis
Example 3: contrast
Example 4: illustration

Paragraph Sequencing

Writers must be sure that their paragraphs follow the steps of
their logic. Usually, you can trace the writer's logic through the
topic sentences of paragraphs.

A topic sentence states the main idea of the paragraph. For
emphasis, this sentence is usually stated at or near the beginning of the paragraph. If the topic sentence is a summary of
the combined implications of a number of examples, it will be
stated last or near the end of the paragraph. Rarely is a topic
sentence located in the middle of the paragraph, since this
would tend to de-emphasize it.

Here's a paragraph you've already seen. Locate the topic
sentence.

....

Jargon is the language of specialists and is appropriate when
writing or speaking to other specialists in the same field. People
conversant in a jargon usually aren't offended by it. But a writer
should never assume a reader's familiarity with jargon. Don't
make the mistake of assuming that "anyone who knows anything about business will know what I mean when I write of
cash cows." Don't bet on it. Jargon tends to be more local than

you think, and many successful executives have never heard of cash cows and would prefer not to.

....

You probably spotted the topic sentence. It's the first sentence. The rest of the paragraph extends and clarifies the point through explanation and specific examples.

In the following passage, the writer places topic sentences effectively both at the beginnings and at the ends of paragraphs. I've italicized these so that you can see the skeleton of the argument's logic.

....

Recently, I met a commercial banker in his fifties who told me the following: "You know, not too long ago all that a commercial banker had to do to generate business was to handle a knife and fork and play golf." That was in the era when banks were regulated and competitors were few. *Today, bankers play an entirely different game.*

The banking industry has changed radically. I suspect that the often-used expression "stuffy banker" will quickly die out from usage, simply because there will no longer be room for this type of individual. The traditional, relatively passive, genteel commercial bankers will, of necessity, be replaced by a tough new breed of bankers. What do I mean by "tough?"

I mean tough in the sense that to make money these people will have to work much harder and be much smarter than their predecessors. The easy days of banking are over. Today, we need men and women who not only have good social skills but who also have superb technical skills coupled with outstanding selling ability.

....

A summary of these sentences yields the writer's argument: Because the banking industry is different from the way it used to be, the people who enter it must be different from the bankers of the past.

Let's revisit another paragraph you've seen before.

....

Cyclical sales growth is partially controlled by continuous expansion and sufficient capitalization. Forecasting tools enable the company to plan ahead in order to control costs and protect profit margins. Quality store management and incentive programs also offset downturns to sales and/or margins. Since the company lacks diversification, cyclicality must be partially mitigated by management.

....

Can you find the topic sentence? Probably not. All the sentences are written in such large and general terms that any of them, or none of them, could be topic sentences. Since you cannot locate the main point of the paragraph, it's impossible to determine if there's a sequence of logic from sentence to sentence.

The writer of this paragraph told me that his readers could "infer the meaning." But readers should not have to read your mind. In business writing, the point of a paragraph must be clearly stated and explained. Otherwise the larger logic that's being developed from paragraph to paragraph, as well as the logic within paragraphs, is not apparent to the reader, and he or she won't be able to follow the writer's "trail."

Transitions

Transitions are the signposts that help the reader follow the writer's logical trail. Without them, readers can become confused and disoriented or lose their way.

Some transitions are obvious and straightforward. Looking again at an example you've already seen, notice how the enumerating words *first*, *second*, and *third* make it easier to follow the writer's argument.

As you are aware, a letter was released from this office regarding our new corporate policy of reporting all purchase contracts in excess of ten thousand dollars. To date, we have received no response from the manufacturing facilities. There are a number of possible explanations for this with varying implications.

First, it is possible that $10,000 was an inappropriate level in that most contracts negotiated were under this level. An appropriate response to this problem would be to reassess historic purchasing levels in order to establish an appropriate threshold.

Second, the problem may have resulted from the fact that the letter was released on a date too close to the peak buying season, thus not allowing the respective executives adequate time to assimilate the request into their current purchasing procedures. If this is the case, we should begin to realize the expected benefits of the new directive when the next buying cycle begins.

Third, the problem may represent a message from the purchasing executives that they resent head office tampering with their established routines. In this event, we would need to make them realize the benefits that everyone will gain if they comply with this procedure.

In my opinion, *the first explanation is most likely*. An appropriate course of action at this point would be to arrange a conference of all the purchasing executives to discuss the problem as a group. Such a conference would also allow us to talk to each executive.

This example also illustrates another important principle: the beginning of paragraphs is usually the place to achieve a smooth transition from the previous paragraph. There will be times, however, that you'll use the end of the paragraph to provide the linkage into the next paragraph. For example:

....

I suspect the often-used expression "stuffy banker" will quickly die out from usage, simply because there will no longer be room for this type of individual. The traditional, relatively passive, genteel commercial banker will, of necessity, be replaced by a tough new breed of bankers. *What do I mean by "tough"?*

I mean tough in the sense that to make money these people will have to work much harder and be much smarter than their predecessors. The easy days of banking are over.

....

Picking up the thread of an idea stated at the end of one paragraph and continuing it into the next provides the needed transition.

A number of words help writers show connections between sentences and paragraphs. In using them, writers must consider carefully what kinds of relationships these words show and then what kind of relationship their particular context calls for. As an aid, here is a list of some of these words, along with the kinds of relationships they signify.

Transitional Words	*What Is Signified*
Moreover, furthermore, in addition, besides, first, second, finally	Continuing a point or presenting detail
Therefore, because, according, consequently, thus, hence, as a result, so	Cause and effect relationship
Similarly, here again, likewise, in comparison	Comparison

Yet, conversely, whereas, nevertheless, on the other hand, however, nonetheless, but	Contrast
Although, if, unless, provided that	Condition
For example, in particular, in this case, for instance	Illustration
Formerly, after, when, meanwhile, sometimes, subsequently	Time sequence
Indeed, in fact, in any event	Emphasis
That is, in other words, as has been stated	Repetition

The key to using transitions effectively is recognizing the thought processes that they signal.

Now you're going to have the opportunity to write several paragraphs in which you develop an argument. Remember: sequence the paragraphs logically and link them with transitions.

Exercise: Developing an Argument

Write three paragraphs in which you ask your boss for a raise. Assume that the raise is overdue and that you deserve it. Develop your case on the basis of *reason and logic*—for example, show the just causes that you should get the raise, present examples of your good work, compare your work in the past with your current performance to show that you've improved—whatever content makes sense for your case. *Do not* use emotional arguments such as "I need a raise because I've got a new baby on the way." We'll consider these kinds of strategies in the next lesson.

When you've finished your paragraphs, go back and underline:

- *at least one example* of illustration, comparison or contrast, and cause and effect analysis. It's almost certain that you will have used each thought process at least once.
- *one transitional bridge* between *two* of the paragraphs.
- the *topic sentence in each paragraph.*

Suggested Revision: Developing an Argument

Although I can't give you direct commentary on your writing, I'm providing a sample of another person's argument along with commentary on some of the developmental techniques used, an example of a transition, and the placement of the topic sentences. I also suggest that you show your work to a friend, asking him or her to respond in light of the principles discussed in the lesson.

....

Sample Response

I've now been working with this consulting company for almost a year. During that time, I've designed and taught four major courses for two new clients, Pemper Corporation and Lifko Associates. Not only did I receive uniformly excellent feedback from participants in all sessions, but you yourself told me that "Jane Adamson at Pemper said Rachel Johnston came in, psyched out this company, and delivered the kind of quality product that hasn't been seen around here in at least ten years."

As a result of these contributions, I believe I should be considered for a raise. When we first began our association, we agreed that my per diem rate would be $200 less than my usual rate so that I could have the chance to work with you on a wider variety of projects than had been possible for me alone. Part of our verbal agreement also entailed my performing free course-needs analyses to help you get more business. My understanding was, however, that once we had built up enough business, you would raise my per diem rate to an appropriate fee. To date, I have helped you gain two new clients, yet I am still being paid a substandard per diem fee. I believe an appropriate raise would be $400 added to the per diem rate—$200 to bring me up to my normal rate plus a $200 merit addition.

I must also require payment in the future for the time I spend on needs analyses, and will bill you at the per diem rate I charge for my other services. As you know, the last needs analysis we did for Lifko Associates required two full days of interviewing and three days to analyze the data and write the client's report. That was five days of my time I gave you gratis. I realize that you don't mind doing free needs analyses for clients—you own the company and can make up the money in terms of what you charge the client if you get the business. But I cannot be asked to work as if I'm a partner when I'm really an employee.

Examples of Paragraph Development Processes

- Cause and effect analysis: "As a result of these contributions, I believe I should be considered for a raise." (In fact, the basic argument throughout is based on cause and effect reasoning: Because I helped you build up more business, I should get a raise.)
- Contrast: "I realize that you don't mind doing free needs analyses for clients—you own the company and can make up the money in terms of what you charge the client if you get the business. But I cannot be asked to work as if I'm a partner when I'm really an employee."
- Illustration: "Jane Adamson at Pemper said Rachel Johnston came in, psyched out this company, and delivered the kind of quality product that hasn't been seen around here in at least ten years."

Example of Transitional Bridge

- "As a result of these contributions . . ." forms a transition from paragraph one to paragraph two.

Placement of Topic Sentences

- The topic sentences are the *first* sentences of each paragraph.

Emotional Arguments: The Art of Persuasion

Emotional argumentation is not as common in business writing as in other types of writing. Generally, the subject of profit and loss is best looked at in the light of hard reason and factual observation; emotions can cloud the subject unnecessarily. Yet there are occasions where emotion plays an important and rightful part in business writing. The key is recognizing these opportunities when they present themselves and knowing your audience well enough to take advantage of those opportunities.

Perhaps one of the most famous examples of recognizing the moment for emotion and knowing how to evoke it from an audience is illustrated in Marc Antony's famous funeral oration in *Julius Caesar*.

Shakespeare dramatizes this occasion by having one of Caesar's murderers, Brutus, speak his eulogy first over the fallen leader. Brutus appeals to the reasonableness of the citizens, pointing out that Caesar's ambition was becoming a threat to the republic: "If then that friend demand why Brutus rose against Caesar, this is my answer: Not that I loved Caesar less, but that I loved Rome more. Had you rather Caesar were living, and die all slaves, than that Caesar were dead, to live all free men?"

Taking advantage of the opportunity to speak after Brutus, Marc Antony calls Brutus's motives into question and whips up the crowd's emotions about the assassination:

....

> Here, under leave of Brutus and the rest—
> For Brutus is an honorable man;
> So are they all, all honorable men—
> Come I to speak in Caesar's funeral.
> He was my friend, faithful and just to me:
> But Brutus says he was ambitious;
> And Brutus is an honorable man.
> He hath brought many captives home to Rome,
> Whose ransoms did the general coffers fill:
> Did this in Caesar seem ambitious?
> When that the poor have cried, Caesar hath wept;
> Ambition should be made of sterner stuff.

....

Antony's oration shows a knowledge of human psychology. He speaks of his own experience that Caesar was a just and honest friend. While you might argue that logically this says little about Caesar's fairness to the citizens, this same kind of argument is often used with the same success in everyday life: "X is a nice person and a good friend of mine; therefore, he would be a good candidate for this job." A personal endorsement always carries emotional weight. Similarly, the example "When that the poor have cried, Caesar hath wept" is strictly hearsay. But if you believe the speaker, as the crowd in Rome believed Antony, you'll be likely to believe the example.

Antony's speech illustrates that, on certain occasions, an emotional argument may be more effective than a rational one. It also illustrates that emotion is best used as an argumentative technique only if it is genuine. Although Antony probably slanted his evidence, his love for Caesar was genuine, and that feeling comes through in his speech. Emotion, when it's real and not manufactured, can be powerfully persuasive.

Let's look at a letter we've seen before—the letter seeking political action on the PATH strike. You saw the letter written first in a passive, weak style. You saw it revised into active voice, which gave it more stylistic strength and made its message more direct and clear.[1] Now look at the letter someone actually wrote when his frustration with the strike was at its peak:

Dear Governor:

I am writing to express the outcry of 70,000 hot, tired, angry New Jersey residents who try to commute every day to New York.

We are incensed over half-hearted negotiations between the Port Authority and representatives of 170 carmen.

One hundred seventy carmen!

You have declared publicly that the PATH fare must be kept at thirty cents for the welfare of New Jersey residents. The hundreds of neighbors I see every day join me in imploring you to use your office to:

1. Announce your support of a fare increase to seventy-five cents per ride. Even one dollar as on the New York subway is not unreasonable.
2. Compel the Port Authority and union officials to engage in around-the-clock negotiations to reach an immediate agreement.

---

[1]See Chapter 3, p. 49.

As long as the carmen are making nearly as much money staying at home as going to work, *why would they settle*? As long
as the Port Authority is reporting a smaller deficit by not operating the PATH than by operating it, especially at a measly thirty
cents, *why would they settle*? Clearly, they need some firm,
pointed impetus from you.

Transport of New Jersey has made an honorable attempt to provide emergency alternative service. By their own admission,
though, their efforts will never match the speed and comfort of
below-the-surface trans-Hudson service. Record-breaking temperatures have made the added commuting hours of the last 59
days nearly unbearable.

If you truly wish to aid the welfare of New Jersey residents,
intervene urgently. All 70,000 commuters and their families will
be immensely grateful.

....

How does the writer express his emotion? First, he chooses
words that are much more richly connotative and expressive
than the words used in the other letters: *outcry, incensed, half-
hearted, imploring, measly*. He gives concrete examples to explain his reasoning that the strike is more likely to continue
than be settled: "As long as the carmen are making nearly as
much money staying at home as going to work, *why would
they settle*? As long as the Port Authority is reporting a smaller
deficit by not operating the PATH than by operating it,
expecially at a measly thirty cents, *why would they settle*?" He
vividly illustrates the effects of the strike on commuters: "hot,
tired, angry" people for whom "record-breaking temperatures
have made the added commuting hours of the last 59 days
nearly unbearable."

This letter also shows the writer's knowledge of his audience's
psychology. Nothing strikes more terror to the heart of a politi-
cian than unhappy, frustrated voters who blame your political
inattention for their problems. By asking the governor directly

for "firm, pointed impetus" in the form of "using his office" to "announce" and "compel" change, the writer implicitly challenges the reader to show that he will use his political power in a real crisis and not avoid the issue.

Perhaps the most important thing this letter illustrates is that the best use of emotion is in the service of a good cause. I mentioned some examples from *Julius Caesar* and from everyday business life where emotion may be effective but may not always be in the service of a good cause. History shows that Julius Caesar was indeed on the road to becoming a dictator and destroying the Roman Republic. I'm sure you can think of occasions in your own life when you've known hearsay and cronyism to triumph over reason, fact, and truth. I cannot teach you to recognize a good cause. I can only trust that you will do so.

What, then, are some occasions in business that might rightfully call an emotional argument into play? Perhaps one might be a letter or memo in which you're trying to get action on something that you perceive as unfair, hopelessly messed up, or in need of immediate attention to improve it. If you feel strongly enough about the situation, then letting your emotion show will definitely grab the readers' attention and have some kind of an effect on them. A letter of resignation, a "vision statement" to the troops to rally them behind a new corporate strategy, a letter addressing a commonly shared inequity in the organization on which you're attempting to get political action—these are some forms that an emotional argument might take.

Clearly, showing emotion is a risky and often inappropriate technique in business writing. As mentioned, it can tend to cloud the real factual issues of a situation. Unfortunately, enough of this happens in the routine performance of business without anyone's attempting to add to it. Emotion may put readers off, offend them, or, if they disagree with your position, turn them into potentially dangerous adversaries. For these reasons, most business writers avoid it, especially on paper. If they are going to let their emotions show, they'll do so informally, verbally, and "off the record."

If you're going to be emotional in business writing, always keep in mind these things we've discussed:

1. *Why* you think the occasion calls for an emotional appeal
2. *Whom* you're writing to and what is likely to be psychologically persuasive for them in this particular situation.

Finally, don't try to manufacture emotion. If it's there, you'll know it.

Exercise: Showing Emotion in Business Writing

Rewrite the report in which you asked your boss for a raise. This time, express your feelings about the subject. Your strategy for reaching your reader psychologically will be just as important as the language you choose. Thus before you draft the argument, write a brief sketch of the person you're writing to and include your strategy for reaching him or her psychologically. For example:

....

I'm a woman writing to a person who is highly political and sensitive to events that might potentially cause him or the company trouble. As a result, one major point I need to make is that a man with exactly the same background and qualifications as mine was hired for the same job as mine at a higher salary and at a higher grade level. Mentioning sex discrimination is likely to move him to action.

....

For this strategy to work, *there would have to be truth* in your suggestion that you've been the possible victim of sex discrimination. And you'd really have to know your reader. The strategy above could backfire with a lot of people. It would be most likely to work with an insecure person who knows you've been wronged and would not want you to "make a fuss," or a person who, though political, knows you've been wronged and will have a sense of fair play. While your language would be strong and perhaps threatening for the first reader, you'd use words suggesting the concepts of fairness and equality for the second reader.

Suggested Revision: Showing Emotion in Business Writing

Once again, since I cannot provide you direct commentary on your writing, I'm providing a sample revision. Again, the best response to your work would come from a friend or colleague, particularly one who knows the person or kind of person you're writing for and who can therefore evaluate your strategy.

The revision here is of the argument you saw in the exercise on pages 156–157. This time, the writer shows emotion. The description of the reader is:

I'm writing for a boss who is fair and reasonable, but who has allowed his desire for profit to cloud his judgment. Part of the reason he has neglected my raise is that he has a number of other consultants like me working for him who are willing to do needs analyses gratis and take lower per diem wages than mine in order to break into the business. I need to emphasize something we both know: I'm more valuable than these people because I can do difficult assignments that they cannot do and because I have actually helped him build up business while these people have not. I may have to threaten to quit. I am *absolutely* sure that he would not want me to do that. He knows there are a number of his competitors who would love to have my services.

....

Sample Revision

When I first started working with your company, we agreed that my per diem rate would be $200 less than my usual rate so that I could have the chance to work with you on a wider variety of projects than had been possible for me alone. We also agreed, however, that if the kinds of specialized courses I design actually brought in more business, I would be raised to my usual rate plus a merit addition.

I've been working for you for almost a year now. As you know, the Pemper and Lifko accounts are a direct result of my sales and design skills. Yet I am still being paid a substandard per diem fee. I'm so upset about this that I'm on the verge of leaving. We agreed, after all, that I would be rewarded when I delivered on my promise to help you get some new clients. I've honored my end of the bargain. I think a raise that brings me up to my standard rate plus a $200 merit addition is certainly justified now.

I will also have to start charging you per diem for doing needs analyses. As things stand now, I am being asked to give large blocks of my time gratis. I realize that you and the other freelance consultants who work for you always do clients' needs analyses at no charge, but in the future I must require payment for the time I spend on this work. I can understand that you don't mind doing free needs analyses—you own the company and can make up the money you lose on this service in terms of what you charge the client once they buy the course. And if other people want to give away their labor to break into consulting, that's their decision. But those people clearly have not made the contribution that I have made to the company nor is there any chance that they will be able to do so; we both know that they don't have the skills.

I have helped and will continue to help you *increase* your profits. Talent, after all, is the "bottom line" in this business. But I cannot be asked to share those talents for nothing!

....

Commentary: Showing Emotion in Business Writing

Even though this argument is only moderately emotional, I think you can imagine how risky it would be to write it—even for the kind of reader described. You'd have to be dead sure your services were as valuable to the boss as this person thinks they are. Otherwise, you might find yourself out of a job.

The point to remember is: always weigh *carefully* the risks of emotionalism in business writing.

8

Opening and Closing the Report

Introductory Techniques: Briefing

Sometimes the reader needs to be given background information or apprised of a special situation giving rise to the memorandum before receiving the bottom-line message. I call this kind of introduction *briefing* in the sense of "giving precise instructions or essential information."

You're already familiar with the process of briefing whether you know it or not. When you invite your in-laws for dinner, you might brief them about the arrival time, whether the children will be there to greet them, what you're planning to serve, or how many other guests are invited. Commentators on the evening news often report that the President's press secretary met with him to "brief" him before a news conference. This means the press secretary armed him with vital facts, statistics, and other information to use in fielding reporters' questions.

You might reasonably ask, why can't a memorandum simply begin, "I've decided," "I've concluded," or "I recommend?" Why not just start with the lead or hooking paragraph, the way newspaper writers do?

You *can* in some cases and *not* in others. The briefing *prepares the reader to understand your purpose for having written the memo.* That is, if readers are not familiar with the situation that gave rise to the memo, you may have to take time to brief them on the necessary background. If they have the background, the briefing may be no more than a simple phrase to remind them of the occasion, such as:

···

"As you requested"

···

169

or

....

"In light of . . . " (followed by brief statement of situation giving rise to the memo)

....

If you know the reader knows why the memo is being written and he or she is a very informal, "get-to-the point" sort of person, you can simply begin, "I recommend" or "I've decided" and dispense with briefing.

Here is an example of a memorandum seeking approval of a customer's request for a loan. It was written by a junior credit officer to a credit officer several steps above him in the approval hierarchy. Here's how the memo would open *without briefing:*

....

TO: Approving Officer

FROM: Junior Credit Officer

SUBJECT: *Approval of $200M Line of Credit to Sure Lure Company*

I recommend we extend the $200M line of credit to Sure Lure Company with the following restriction:

- Under a borrowing base formula, lend 90% against receivables that are current or no more than 90 days past due.

The restriction protects the bank from the line being used to:

- support unsold inventory, or
- finance poor-quality receivables.

....

If the officer knows the company and what it intends to use the loan to finance, he or she might appreciate such a direct opening. However, as often happens in large organizations, if the approving officer does not know the customer or the purpose of the loan, this opening may seem presumptuous. "How am I supposed to know what this is all about?" might be the reaction. In such a case, the reader would expect to be *prepared* to understand the recommendation. Even though the body of the report would undoubtedly explain the reasons for the decision, the opening might put the reader in an unreceptive frame of mind to hear the writer's argument.

In short, briefings serve two purposes. One is telling the readers what they need to know or emphasizing the importance of something they already know so that they can understand your main message. The second is beginning the process of influencing the reader to understand your point of view or agree with your position, decision, plan, or recommendation.

Thus before you write a briefing, you must consider:

- *Whom* you're writing to, *why* they need background, and *what* information they need to know.
- What *tone* is likely to be most appropriate for the readers and most likely to help them respond to your writing in the way you would wish.

Once you've answered the questions *who, what*, and *why*, you should have a good sense of what information you need to give the reader. Be careful that you do not present a lot of facts that may be interesting but do not really help prepare readers for the case explained in the memo. Nothing is more annoying than a report that starts off with a turgidly written lump of ill-digested or poorly organized facts and statistics. The readers' first impulse will probably be to trash the memo.

Remember: first impressions count in writing, too. If one part of the memo has to be exquisitely well written, it is the briefing. Edit, rewrite, and edit again until you've made it a polished gem.

In addition to selecting information the reader needs to know, briefings should begin to set the stage for the emotions and attitudes you want the reader to have toward your message. Good examples of this kind of preparation occur in all major art forms: movies, television, plays, and operas. For example, in movies and television, we may scarcely be aware of the effect background music is having on us, but it is definitely establishing a mood. Think of the opening of "The Twilight Zone," "The Alfred Hitchcock Show," or "The Pink Panther" and how the music prepares the audience for the mood of the films. A visual analog of theme music is the credits themselves and the way they're presented at the beginning of a film. All these devices are used to influence the audience and help them become receptive to the experience they're about to have. Finally, overtures and preludes have long been used to prepare the audience for the mood of the play or opera to come.

Similarly, you deliver a subliminal message to the reader in the briefing as well as an informational message. This subliminal message is called *tone,* which may be defined as the secondary message you wish to communicate.

In our everyday lives, we are very careful not only about *what* we say, but *how* we say it. When speaking with people, we consider the impact our tone of voice might have on them. In writing, you must also consider what impact your written tone of voice might have on the reader's feelings.

When you're speaking, of course, tone is really *tone.* It means the tonality or inflection you give words with the voice. A simple sentence such as "Okay, you're right" can be said in tones of agreement, incredulousness, frustration, or in a way that puts the other person down.

In writing, you will use the tones and colors of words themselves to get your reader in a receptive frame of mind to read your report. A writer's palette or instrumentation consists mostly of:

- adjectives
- adverbs
- the connotation and denotation of words
- transitions

Consider the different tonal impact of these four sentences:

- The company has a $300,000 debt.
- The company has only a $300,000 debt.
- The company owes a major debt of $300,000.
- Although the company owes a $300,000 debt, it remains a good risk for more loans.

The last sentence also illustrates that the kinds of explanations given—"it remains a good risk for more loans"—help establish the writer's tone.

In sum, the briefing helps get readers in a receptive frame of mind to receive your communication and helps them have the attitudes that will be most beneficial to your purpose in the written document. At the same time, the briefing supplies necessary facts or emphasizes the importance of information the reader may already know but that is especially important to your case.

Briefings generally take one of two forms. One is a covering memo that prepares the reader for something it's attached to. Here's an example:

TO: Managers

FROM: Joe Jones, System Consultant

SUBJECT: First Aid Kit

Have you ever logged on to your terminal or PC expecting to see your LOFS main menu but instead find the message "Reconnected"? Or maybe you hit the enter key and got no response at all?

Well, the answers to these and other perplexing systems quirks are being addressed in a VM First Aid Kit. The attached kit contains a list of frequent problems and their solutions for both the PC and the terminal.

A LOFS reference card will also be available in September. It will contain some helpful information and instructions on using LOFS major functions.

If you have any questions about the First Aid Kit, call Jane or Kate in the Info Center on extension 7790 or 7650.

Cover memos are often used to introduce an attachment or summarize the findings of a longer research report.

A second common form of briefing is an introductory paragraph or paragraphs that prepare the readers for the report to come. Here's the lead excerpt you saw earlier preceded by briefing:

TO: Approving Officer

FROM: Junior Credit Officer

SUBJECT: *Approval of $200M Line of Credit to Sure Lure Company*

Sure Lure is an old, family-run fishing lure manufacturing company. The company increased its sales in 1987 by 16% to $9,717,940, placing it tenth among the top ten lure manufacturers. Recent plant modernization is likely to keep the company among the leaders in this steadily growing and highly competitive industry, which supplies the third most popular participation sport in the U.S.

The company plans to use the requested line of credit to enter the retail market. This is a new market for Sure Lure, which has always sold to regional wholesalers. This line would allow the company to:

- increase stock in anticipation of new sales, or
- extend credit to new retail customers.

I recommend that we extend the $200M line of credit to Sure Lure with the following restriction:

- Under a borrowing base formula, lend 90% against receivables that are current or no more than 90 days past due.

The restriction protects the bank from the line being used to:

- support unsold inventory, or
- finance poor-quality receivables.

....

Notice that the writer has been very selective about what information is presented in the briefing. Without going into a lot of detail, he selects a few key facts to paint the picture of a moderately successful company (tenth among the top ten) in a promising industry ("steadily growing and highly competitive"). A key adverb within a judgmental statement should predispose the reader to view a fact about the company as a predictor of future success: "Recent plant modernization [fact] is *likely* [adverb] to *keep the company among the leaders*" [judgment]. He also briefs the reader about the purpose for which the loan was requested—one of the first things any credit officer wants to know. Clearly, he knows the type of person he's writing for, even if he may not know the individual personally.

Once again, the key to writing effective briefings is thinking about the readers, their attitudes, their knowledge, and their needs. You may actually find it easier to influence your readers in business writing than essayists or polemists who attempt to influence a general audience.

For example, recall the excerpt by Germaine Greer at the beginning of this book.[1] When she attempts to persuade readers to look past feminine stereotypes, her tone and strategies of persuasion will not work for everybody. The range of personalities who will read her argument is simply too varied and diverse for anyone to reach.

In business writing, however, you often know personally those to whom you're writing. Even if you don't know them personally, as might be the case of the junior credit officer writing to someone higher up in the approval chain, you'll probably know who they are and what they would expect to see in your report simply by virtue of their job or function in the company. You can "fine-tune" your briefing and arguments accordingly.

Exercise: Briefing

Read the following briefing paragraph:

....

> This memorandum marks the official beginning of the 1988 Planning and Budgeting Process for the department. As many of you have heard, our approach this year will be significantly different from previous years. Each area will be

---

[1] See Chapter 1, pp. 4–5.

asked to use a new procedure to plan and write their budget reports. This memo will explain the steps of the new procedure and how to document them.

....

This briefing appears to be written for readers who have heard that a new procedure is coming. Nothing in the writing indicates that the writer expects any resistance from the readers toward the procedure or the contents of the memorandum.

Now read the following descriptions of two different types of readers who are going to receive this memorandum. Then rewrite the paragraph above for *each* of the different audiences. Use language and explanations that will influence them to be receptive to the report. Assume that the basic information contained in the paragraph above will be sufficient for each of these audiences. The descriptions will provide you any other information you might need.

....

Briefing Situation 1

You are writing to a group of managers who are not aware that the Central Comptroller's Area wants them to use a new procedure for the 1988 Planning and Budgeting Process. They are likely to be unpleasantly surprised by the new requirement. They may think this method is unnecessarily detailed and will make preparation of the budget more difficult than it needs to be. You'll have to emphasize that since company expenses and staff levels have been rising significantly over the last three years, a more precise budget plan is needed from each department so that the Central Comptroller's Area can track all company expenses more closely. The procedure will also enable each department to get a much clearer picture of its expenses than they've had in the past.

Your revision: _____

_____

_____

_____

_____

_____

_____

_____

_____

_____

_____

_____

_____

_____

....

Briefing Situation 2

You are writing to a group of managers who actually participated in helping you prepare the new procedure that must be
used to submit their 1988 budgets. Several managers con-
sulted with you about the problems creating the need for a
new procedure before you wrote it. Several other managers
read drafts of the procedure that you submitted to them and
gave you many useful suggestions for ways to improve and
simplify it. As a result, you were able to draft a procedure that
is clearly written and will be easy to use.

Your revision: _____

_____

_____

_____

_____

_____

....

Suggested Revisions: Briefing

Once again, since I can't give you direct commentary on your writing, I'm providing sample revisions with analytical commentary on the language and techniques used to influence the readers. I again suggest that you show your work to a friend, asking him or her to respond in light of the principles discussed in the lesson.

....

Sample Revision: Briefing Situation 1

We all know that company expenses and staff levels have been rising significantly over the last three years. As a result, the Central Comptroller's Area has asked each department to provide them more precise budget plans this year so that they will be able to track overall company expenses more closely. This report will explain exactly how to use the new procedure for preparing the budget that the Comptroller's Area has developed. You'll find that the details they're asking you to provide will help you watch your area's expenses more closely, thus benefitting your department as well as the company in general.

....

Comment

The briefing begins by reminding readers of a noncontroversial fact that they all know and will agree with. The writer then explains how this fact has caused the comptrollers to need more precise information in the budgets than they've needed in the past. The writer emphasizes the *causes* leading to the new procedure rather than the effect, the procedure itself. A key adverb, *exactly*, suggests that the report will provide them with precise instructions for using the procedure, which should assuage some fears they may have about having to do the budgets a different way. The briefing closes by emphasizing that the departments as well as the company in general will benefit from the change—a strategy that should further motivate the readers to want to use the procedure.

Sample Revision: Briefing Situation 2

Once again, I'd like to thank each of you for your many helpful suggestions about the best way to standardize the new budget procedure for all the departments. I think you'll find that the procedure explained below is clear and easy to use, primarily because of your editing and ideas for ways to improve and simplify it.

Comment

A "thank you" and a pat on the back for a job well done are always appreciated, yet these simple gestures of common courtesy are too often neglected in the business world. The paragraph also centers on the contribution the readers made to the procedure, not the work the memo writer did in writing the actual procedure. This strategy, which is often called "you-centered" writing as opposed to "I-centered" writing, is almost always a sure motivator and is a favorite strategy of salesmen and sales writers. Let's face it; everyone responds to a compliment, especially if it is sincere and deserved.

Frontloading and Signing Off

Whether you elect to summarize your conclusions in a lead paragraph or hook your readers into the report, the intent of these openings is the same: capturing the readers' interest immediately. This principle is often referred to as *frontloading*. In fact, the principle of frontloading informs most written business communication at every level: the sentence, the paragraph, the overall organization of the report, and the title, which in memorandums takes the form of the *subject title*.[2]

People who first join the business world right out of college or high school are often not very conscious of the principle of frontloading. They are more comfortable with the principle of building up their case slowly in the familiar essay pattern first proposed by Aristotle: introduction, body, conclusion or, as the great Greek put it, beginning, middle, and end. This is the form generally used to explore a thesis. In the academic essay, a proposition or original idea (the thesis) is stated in the introduction, explained, illustrated, or justified in the body, and then reiterated more forcefully at the end.

Even though the pace of introduction and argument may be slower in essays than in reports, essays do observe one important frontloading principle: *the thesis is stated up front*. If you learned to do this in your academic writing classes, you're halfway home to being a good business writer.

In my opinion—and here I differ from a number of management communication theorists I know—the form of reports and memorandums is really very similar to the Aristotelian essay. The two major differences are the modifications business writers make in opening and closing a report.

---

[2]Sherry Sweetnam gives a good discussion of frontloading strategies in her book, *The Executive Memo: A Guide to Persuasive Business Communications* (New York: John Wiley & Sons, 1986), pp. 78–82.

Frontloading Techniques

In business writing, you will most often state your bottom-line conclusion, recommendation, decision, or judgment in the first paragraph. You do so because the content of most everyday business writing is not controversial or provocative. If you have reason to think an introduction is needed to ease the reader into your bottom-line message, that introduction can be specific and concise and can be fine-tuned to the readers for whom the report was written. Thus the briefing is very often combined with a lead or hooking opening into one paragraph. On the other hand, essays written for a general audience, such as academic essays, often require longer introductions that brief readers on a variety of subjects and issues to prepare them to hear the thesis.

Even a hooking opening, if carefully inspected, usually contains a major conclusion or idea. Look again at an example you saw before:

....

When you read how many discrepancies I found when I reviewed this audit, I think you'll agree *we should review audit reports with our auditors before publication* [conclusion italicized].

....

Although an important part of the bottom-line message was reserved for the end of this report—the specific recommendations for how to conduct the review with the auditors—the most important single idea in the report still found its way up front. One theorist has described this principle as "the pyramid principle," meaning that the report starts with its most important concept or idea at the highest level of abstraction and works its way down through supporting ideas at lower levels of abstraction.[3] Thus the report is shaped like a pyramid. This

---

[3]Barbara Minto, *The Pyramid Principle: Logic in Writing and Thinking* (United States of America: Minto International Inc., 1982), pp. 8–11.

theory is a way of visualizing the idea of the thesis and the pattern of "most important to least important" order.

Like essays, reports and memorandums also have titles that pinpoint the main message up front. In essays, the title is given first, then the author's name, and then the essay is presented; an essay is, of course, written for anyone who chooses to read it. Reports and memorandums, since they are written to specific people, generally designate who those people are before they specify who the writer is and what the title is. They also record the date they were written. As a result, memo headings have four parts:

March 7, 1988

TO: Jay Jones

FROM: Alice Smith

SUBJECT: *Evaluation of Program Design*

The best subject titles, just like the titles of essays, tell the reader something specific about the purpose or content of the report. They should also grab the readers' attention and pique their interest. For example:

Uninformative Subject Title	*Informative Subject Title*
1. Sure Lure, Inc.	1. Approval of $3MM Line of Credit to Sure Lure, Inc.
2. Progress Report	2. Progress Report on Centralized Purchasing

3. Program Evaluation Findings	3. Findings of Program Evaluation
	or
	Why We Need to Hire an Instructional Designer

Often a good subject title will offer a reduced version of the report's main point, as the Sure Lure example illustrates. If the subject title confines itself to the general topic of the report, as in the second example, you must still describe the specific universe of that topic: a progress report *about what*?

The first revision of the third example illustrates a simple frontloading technique: put the key concept—*Findings*—first, not last. The second revision states a reduced version of the report's main recommendation.

You may recall seeing one of these subject titles before. Let me refresh your memory.

....

Subject: *Findings of Program Evaluation*

I have just completed the first part of the evaluation you requested that I do of our Financial Analysis Preparatory Program. So that I could evaluate the quality of our courses from the student's standpoint, I took three courses our department has been offering for several years: Capital Markets, International Finance, and Corporate Finance. I also took and passed all the exams. The courses, however, were not a totally productive learning experience because their learning objectives were far too broad and ambitious in scope given (1) the entering knowledge of the average learner and (2) the time allotted for each course.

....

The last sentence states the writer's major conclusion about the program, but the recommendation based on that conclusion was reserved for the end of the report. If the first paragraph had stated or prepared the reader for the recommendation more specifically than this one does, the more specific subject title would be appropriate. In this case, since the reader will probably be surprised by the recommendation, the writer presents her major conclusion and reasoning before proposing a course of action. Thus she elected the more general subject title.

Here's how the writer might recast her first paragraph to dovetail with the more specific subject title:

....

Subject: *Why We Need to Hire an Instructional Designer*

My participation as a student in our Financial Analysis Preparatory Program has led me to some surprising conclusions. The courses we offer now are far too broad and ambitious in scope given (1) the entering knowledge of the average learner and (2) the time allotted for each course. In short, the overall design of the curriculum is flawed, and we should hire an instructional designer to help us redesign the program.

....

This opening paragraph is more powerful than the other one because the writer leads with her trump card, the recommendation, and summarizes her whole case. Once again, whether you elect your most powerful opening or a slower presentation of the case depends on *the person or persons you're writing to*. If, for example, you knew your readers had participated in designing this program you're criticizing, you'd be unwise to tell them up front that their design is flawed and you think a professional needs to clean it up.

We've already discussed sentences and paragraphs, but let me reiterate a couple of important points. First, many of the editorial techniques for streamlining sentences that we have studied are aimed at satisfying the business reader's desire to read reports as quickly and easily as possible. Consider these two sentences:

....

1. As a result of new regulations governing personal loans, we cannot give Mr. Jones the $5000 he requested.
2. We cannot give Mr. Jones the $5000 he requested because of new regulations governing personal loans.

....

The second sentence is more direct than the first because the main point is frontloaded at the beginning. Business readers appreciate directness. They want to grasp main points quickly and move on.

This same impatience to glean the most important information quickly causes most business readers to prefer reports written in paragraphs that *state the topic sentence first*. They also prefer short, pointed paragraphs rather than long expository paragraphs. Short paragraphs (three or four sentences) with frontloaded topic sentences help readers move briskly and easily through the report. Reports written this way are also easier to scan.

Signing Off

A more striking difference between memorandums and essays is their endings. Closing a memo is different from concluding an essay. Essays end with a more powerful statement of the writer's thesis than the one he or she began with. This added gravity and "conclusiveness" generally come from the writer's desire to leave readers with the thesis in the most memorable and convincing way possible.

Reports and memorandums, on the other hand, generally close with a statement of the kind of response the writer wants from readers. Or, as we've discussed, they may close with a course of action the writer wants to propose to the readers. Here are some examples:

....

- We'll need to meet as soon as possible to reach a formal contract agreement by April 1, 1988.

- I need your decision in writing on this proposal by March 1, 1988, so that we can begin formal negotiations with the customer.

- Please call me at 832–1102 if you have any questions about following the procedure I've outlined.

- I believe a professional instructional designer could help us clarify our needs so that we would be able to produce more relevant and successful courses than the ones I attended. Since our boss has been talking for a long time about up-grading these courses, this seems like the right time to give her an action plan to start the ball rolling. Could we set a date sometime next week to put together a full set of recom-mendations? I'd also like to discuss some other reactions I had to the courses I took.

....

Closing a report or memorandum should be a good bit sim-pler than concluding an essay. One thing to avoid, however, is signing off in a formulaic or useless way. This means asking for a response that isn't really a response or trying to say something nice that doesn't actually relate to the memo or its purpose. Some examples are:

....

- I want to thank you in advance for your cooperation. (You're assuming the readers will cooperate—maybe they won't. And you're not specifying what kind of "cooperation" you want.)

- Please let me know your decision at your earliest convenience. (If you give readers this kind of leeway, they may feel no urgency to get back to you—ever!)

- Thank you for your attention. (Again, you're not being specific enough about the kind of response you want from the readers. This is like thanking them for reading the memo.)

....

If you're not recommending action or don't really want a response from readers other than for them to read the report or memo, *stop* at the end of the explanation section. You don't have to repeat your main points or thank them for reading the memo. If your organization was clear and your writing readable, readers should have found the report an informative and, at the very least, painless experience.

Exercise: Frontloading and Action Closings

1. Since asking for a raise is one of those more provocative issues you sometimes have to write about in business, you may have found yourself working up your case slowly or preparing your reader in some other way before actually asking for the raise. Now rewrite the opening paragraph of your request for a raise and *frontload your message*. In other words, state specifically in the first paragraph that you want the raise. You may also want to summarize the main reasons you think you deserve the raise.

Preface this paragraph with a subject title that dovetails with your message. Be sure to observe the principle of frontloading in the subject title as well as in the paragraph itself.

2. Write a closing for your request for a raise that proposes a course of action or asks for a response from the readers. Be specific about what you want the readers to do after having read your memo. Don't just say something vaguely polite or thank them for reading the memo.

Suggested Revisions: Frontloading and Action Closings

Once again, I'm offering suggested revisions instead of direct commentary on your writing. Again, I strongly suggest that you show your work to a colleague who knows the person or persons you're writing to. Ask him or her to help you evaluate your writing in light of the principles we discussed in this lesson.

....

1. *Subject: My Raise*
   In view of my recent contributions to this company's sales, I believe I deserve a raise. As you know, the Pemper and Lifko accounts are a direct result of my sales and design skills. We also agreed when I first started working here that if my specialized courses actually brought in more business, I would be raised to my usual per diem rate and receive a merit addition as well.

....

(Note: Whether you use the frontloaded approach or work up your case more slowly, your success in gaining the raise will ultimately rest on *how valid your readers think your argument is*. In this case, will they be persuaded by the writer's argument that her contributions to sales are as significant as she says they are?)

....

2.   I'd like to discuss this with you personally as soon as possible. Since I will be in the office Monday and Wednesday of next week, can we arrange a meeting for one of those days? I'll call you this Friday to set a time.

....

9

Using Formatting Techniques

Catching the Reader's Eye

If you want your readers to follow you along a logical path, you must act as their guide along the way. Your three major tools for keeping them on the path are readability, organization, and formatting.

Readability of prose style is a writer's major tool for establishing and sustaining the reader's interest, while the organization a writer chooses must follow the pattern that makes sense for presenting the document's content. Format is the way the writer lays out the report visually.

Most writers think of layout as a less important area of writing than logic and prose style, in the same way that artists view painting and sculpture as higher art forms than the crafts of graphic layout and design. However, since we live in a world that has become very sensitive to visual stimuli, business readers, like other modern readers, seem to find format an especially useful aid to readability.

In short, format complements organization to help readers follow the report by *eye* as well as by logic. The various formatting techniques are visual methods of highlighting or emphasizing important points or sections of a report. They can also serve an organizing, classifying, or labeling function. A format can greatly help or hinder the readability of a report.

Formatting is one of the most creative and personal aspects of editing. The variety of techniques that exist may be applied in a number of ways. It's also possible to create a new technique in certain situations. But the final test of a good format is that it helps the reader see logical relationships, emphasizes important points, and in general contributes to the economy and coherence of the writing.

The problem many writers have with format is that they become too attached to one or two techniques rather than thinking about what techniques might genuinely improve the organization and readability of a particular piece of writing. For example, many writers in business today have become enamored of the "bullet point." I once spoke to a vice president of a major corporation who believed that all memos could be constructed entirely in bullet points, obviating the need for him ever to have to write prose again (which he disliked doing).

This is an example of "missing the point" (pun intended) where formatting techniques are concerned. Formatting techniques are not and never will be a substitute for a clear, readable prose style.

Since formatting is part of editing, it is generally the last thing you do after you make your prose style readable. Once you've established the logic your ideas should follow and have made a first attempt at drafting, then you see if subheadings or lists could in some way improve the report's organization and ease of reading.

Sometimes a company suggests or requires a format. Here the danger is to see the format as a formula for writing in which you "fill in the blanks." Generally, a suggested format is only the barest skeletal outline of the logic a memo should take, along with some suggestions concerning the data to be included. In any given structure, many formats within the sections are possible. And you are still faced with the task of achieving coherence from section to section.

Let's take time now to learn about the different kinds of formatting techniques business writers use.

Types of Formatting Techniques

The major types of formatting techniques used in business writing are:

- Instructive and topical subheadings
- Bullet points or lists
- Indenting, underlining, italicizing, and capitalizing
- White space
- Appendices
- T-forms or parallel columns

Instructive and Topical Subheadings

Subheadings are a good way to make large prose sections of reports and memorandums more accessible to readers. First the writer divides the material into small, digestible units. The subheading itself is used to label the content of the units.

There are two types of subheadings: *instructive* and *topical* subheadings.[1]

Topical subheadings identify topics that will be discussed in a section: "The Obligor," "Credit and Marketing," "Recommendations." They are the most general type of subheadings.

Instructive subheadings are more specific than topical subheadings. They identify a theme or state a point that a section will develop. "Company Risks Shrinking Market Share" or "Payment Schedule Not Met" are instructive subheadings.

---

[1] David Ewing, *Writing for Results*, cited in Geraldine Henze's *From Murk to Masterpiece: Style for Business Writing* (Homewood, Illinois: Richard D. Irwin, Inc., 1984), pp. 68–69.

Bullet Points or Lists

Bullet points are a type of list (with a • next to the item instead of a number). Like numbered lists, they can be used only at certain times because lists cannot express relationships among ideas or the relative importance of the ideas. The vice president who thought he could write everything in bullet points was assuming that every reader would have the same logic and sense of priorities as he—an egocentric view, to say the least.

Avoid writing sentences that contain lists unless the lists are very short. Generally, *three* items in a series is all a single sentence can handle, and these items should not be long, complex phrases.

When vertical lists are being used, points should be phrased similarly. Don't mix sentences, phrases, and simple nouns.*

Good Example	*Bad Example*
1. Sell excess inventory	1. Company should sell excess inventory
2. Reduce level of A/Rs	2. A/Rs—reduce
3. Reduce bank's exposure	3. Bank must limit its exposure

Indenting, Underlining, Italicizing, and Capitalizing

These techniques basically help you catch the reader's eye in order to highlight and emphasize points. They should not be overused. For example, if you underline a number of words in a section to achieve emphasis, the eye will become confused and you will achieve exactly the opposite of your objective.

---

*In grammatical terminology, this is called the principle of *parallelism*. Parallelism means using corresponding syntactical forms.

White Space

This is another visual technique to help readers assimilate the written page. It also has a psychological dimension. Most people's hearts sink when they see a page black with type. It looks formidable even if it isn't. Reading a written page where each line runs to the very end of the margin—so much so that the ends of words literally run off the line—is also a very irritating experience. You must *motivate* your readers to find your work accessible and attractive.

Appendices

Webster's defines an appendix as "supplementary matter added at the end of a book." Unlike books, most reports and certainly most memorandums would not be broad enough in scope to warrant appendices. In theory, memorandums are limited in scope and are self-contained.

Occasionally, however, the subject of a report or memorandum warrants extensive research. When writing the explanation section, you may find that, while you do not need to include certain information in the memo's body, it would be helpful to supply that information to the reader in an appendix.

When faced with this situation, the writer must be careful to *cross-reference the information at the exact point in the text where the material would ordinarily have been presented.* A cross-reference is generally noted in parentheses at the point where readers would logically have read the material: for example, (See Appendix I).

An appendix may be referenced in the text in several ways. If there are several appendices, the cross-references can read "See Appendix I," "See Appendix II." Then the appendices themselves, when they are shown at the end of the report, should also each be given an instructive title, such as "Five Changing Demographic Trends of the 80s." An instructive title will direct the reader to each individual appendix's point. If the report's appendix contains only one or two pieces, you can cross-reference by title: See appendix entitled, "Five Changing Demographic Trends of the 80s."

A word of warning: Don't use an appendix as a "dumping ground" for research you've done that the readers do not really need to know. They will not be impressed, nor will they read it, unless it clearly amplifies their knowledge in a relevant way.

T-Forms or Parallel Columns

While parallel columns have always been around, T-forms are a fairly new entrant in the formatting field. The techniques are basically the same: *comparing* or *contrasting* lists of information or points.

The difference is a minor point of layout. You can present your contrasting lists under a T-form or simply line the lists up next to each other using bullet points or numbers. In either case, you'll usually label each column, using either a phrase or a statement that makes clear the purpose of the comparison.

Business memorandums are generally characterized by . . .	*Essays are generally characterized by . . .*
•	•
•	•

Becoming Sensitive to Format

Choosing from this smorgasbord of possible formatting techniques available to writers involves creativity as well as personal choices and preference. There may be a number of techniques that could work well in improving readability. Thus you'll need to become familiar with the choices and how to use them.

To increase your sensitivity to formatting techniques, on the next four pages you'll see presented, side by side, a page of straight prose text on the left page and a formatted page on the right. Be aware of the kinds of techniques used to lay out the page so that the eye can find the point and follow the logic more easily.

Example 1

Now you've learned to state your basic position to your reader in a lead paragraph. Once you've gotten your main points down, you've got to decide how to explain them. Clearly, you've caught only the skeleton of your case in the lead. The rest of the memorandum must "flesh out" that skeleton.

You'll recall we spoke earlier about a couple of thought processes as ways of organizing paragraphs. Let me refresh your memory. Cause and effect analysis means explaining why an event had a certain result or how a certain result stemmed from a particular event. Comparison and contrast means comparing a group of similarities, a group of differences, or a combination of the two in explaining a general point. Now I'll add a definition of a third process. Giving examples is the way we illustrate a general point with concrete details.

....

Example 1 (Revised)

Explaining Your Lead

Now you've learned to state your basic position to your reader in a lead paragraph.

Once you've gotten your main points down, you've got to decide how to explain them. Clearly, you've caught only the skeleton of your case in the lead. The rest of the memorandum must "flesh out" that skeleton.

You'll recall we spoke earlier about a couple of thought processes as ways of organizing paragraphs. Let me refresh your memory:

Cause and effect analysis means explaining why an event had a certain result or how a certain result stemmed from a particular event.

Comparison and contrast means comparing a group of similarities, a group of differences, or a combination of the two in explaining a general point.

Now I'll add a definition of a third process:

Giving examples is the way we *illustrate* a general point with concrete details.

....

Example 2

Business memorandums are generally characterized by direct, to-the-point organization. This means that conclusions, a thesis, or recommendations are stated first, and then followed by supporting arguments or explanation. The memo closes with requests for action or follow-up that the writer wants from the reader.

Essays, on the other hand, are characterized by more leisurely, exploratory organization. Generally, the writer introduces the thesis or main point to whet the reader's appetite. He or she then explores and explains that point and related points in the body of the essay. The piece usually ends in a concluding section in which the writer restates the main point in a more trenchant way.

Memo writers generally do not feel as free to explore subordinate points as do essay writers. Thus the explanation of main points in a memo is usually highly selective and closely related to the main points stated at the beginning of the memo. Essayists have more leeway to explore interesting subordinate issues that, while related to the thesis, may not be of central importance to the arguments supporting the thesis.

The reasons that essayists have more freedom to explore ideas than memo writers stems from whom they're each writing for. Business readers are primarily interested in understanding the report's central message. Readers of essays, however, generally read to gain new ideas or different perspectives on a subject.

Finally, the styles of business writers and essayists usually differ in certain characteristic ways. Business writers favor clear, direct writing. Their major stylistic influences are usually the writing they encounter in newspapers, magazines, and business reports.

Essayists, almost by definition, are often writers with a uniquely interesting way of expressing themselves. Sometimes the way they express themselves is just as important as what they have to say. Their major stylistic influences are usually literary writers—that is, novelists and other essayists.

Example 2 (Revised)

Business memorandums are generally characterized by . . .	*Essays are generally characterized by . . .*
• Direct, to-the-point organization.	• More leisurely, exploratory organization.
• Conclusion or recommendations are stated first, followed by explanation and arguments. The memo closes with a request for any follow-up the writer wants from the reader.	• Main point or thesis is stated first to whet the reader's appetite. The writer then explains that point and related points in the body. Essay usually ends in a concluding section in which the writer restates the main point in a more trenchant way.
• Highly selective explanation of opening points. Pursuing interesting but not absolutely essential subordinate points is generally avoided. Readers are primarily interested in understanding the report's central message.	• More leeway is possible for exploring subordinate ideas that may be related to the essay's thesis. Readers seek to gain new ideas gain new ideas or different perspectives on a subject.
• Style is usually direct, with a minimum amount of stylistic eccentricities and provocative characteristics. The major influence on business writers is usually the kind of writing they encounter in newspapers, magazines, and business reports.	• Essayists are often writers with a uniquely interesting way of expressing themselves. Sometimes the way they express themselves is just as important as what they have to say. Their major stylistic influences are usally literary writers—i.e., novelists and other essayists.

Exercise: Choosing Formatting Techniques

Example 1 used three techniques to format the text: shorter paragraphs, white space, and italics.

Example 2 made extensive use of parallel columns to reformat the prose text. This kind of format usually requires the writer to recast the prose text to achieve readability between the columns. While parallel columns do not have to embody the rule of parallelism as strictly as lists do, writers should try to use approximately the same kind of phrasing and syntactical forms between corresponding points.

Below is a prose example and a list of several formatting techniques you might use to improve its readability. Choose *at least two* of these techniques that you think would work well together if you were to use them to reformat the example. On the worksheet provided, lay out the page using your chosen techniques. You need not fill in every word of prose text unless you want to. If you use subheadings, however, you should write them out.

....

Prose Example

The first thing readers will read in your memorandum is the briefing. Therefore, it's important for you to be able to start them off on the right foot rather than confusing them or putting them off in some way.

In short, good briefings can be distinguished from bad briefings in several outstanding ways.

A good briefing presents only background information that is absolutely necessary for readers to have. Additionally, it sets the stage for the kind of writing style readers can expect and begins the process of influencing and motivating them to want to read the memorandum. If one part of the memo has to be exquisitely well written, it is the briefing. Edit and rewrite until the prose is a polished gem.

A bad briefing generally starts by putting readers off in one or more ways. Sometimes the writer presents a lot of facts that, while interesting, do not really help prepare readers for the case that will ultimately be presented. Sometimes a writer will immediately adopt an inappropriate tone—for example, taking a challenging or confrontational position with a reader who the writer knows is hostile. In such instances, it's better to work the case up more slowly. Even worse is the tendency some writers have to start readers off with a turgidly written lump of ill-digested or poorly organized facts and statistics. Their first impulse, in such cases, is usually to trash the memo. Remember, first impressions count in writing, too.

....

Check off at least two techniques you think you could use together to revise this passage.

_____ white space
_____ instructive subheadings
_____ topical subheadings
_____ underlining or italicizing
_____ capitalizing
_____ T-forms or parallel columns
_____ bullet points

Now lay out the page as you would design it.

Worksheet

Suggested Revisions: Choosing Formatting Techniques

You could probably choose any two formatting techniques and, if they are properly applied, the result would improve the readability of the passage.

In a moment I'll show you two sample revisions. In revision 1, the formatting techniques used were italics, bullet points, and parallel columns.

Revision 2 uses instructive subheadings, identation, white space, italics, and bullet points to format the text. The paragraphs have been shortened and the topic sentences made clearer (see the first sentence of each paragraph).

Although I did not ask you to rewrite the paragraphs, always remember that prose style and organization are still your two most important tools for achieving readability.

As you read these examples and look at your own work, keep in mind that format is one of the most personal and creative aspects of writing. As long as the format makes reading the prose text easier rather than harder, it is probably effective. Format, however, cannot be used as a substitute for writing in prose.

See if your layout is similar to, or perhaps even better than, these two examples.

....

Revision 1

The briefing should . . .	*Be careful the briefing doesn't . . .*
• Present only necessary background information.	• Present a lot of facts that may be interesting but do not really help prepare the reader for the case stated in the memo.

• Help the readers feel receptive to the idea of reading the memo. Tone is an important technique for enticing and motivating the reader to want to read your work.

• Put the reader off in some way—for example, immediately adopting a challenging or confrontational position with readers you know are hostile. Work your case up more slowly.

• Set the stage for the memo's writing style. If one part of the memo has to be exquisitely well written, it is the briefing. Edit! Rewrite! And edit again! Make it a polished gem.

• Start the readers off with a turgidly written lump of ill-digested and poorly organized facts and statistics. Their first impulse will be to trash the memo. Remember, first impressions count in writing, too.

Revision 2

First Impressions Count

The first thing readers will read in your memorandum is the briefing. It's important for you to be able to start them off on the right foot. You want to avoid:

• confusing them
• putting them off in some way

Confusing the Readers

Confusing the readers usually results when you present a lot of irrelevant facts at the beginning of the memorandum. If the briefing does not really help prepare readers for the case that will ultimately be presented, it will confuse them. Even worse is the tendency some writers have to start readers off with a turgidly written lump of ill-digested or poorly organized facts and statistics. In such cases, both form and content are confusing and the readers' first impulse will usually be to trash the memo.

Putting the Readers Off

The writing style of the briefing will either motivate readers to keep reading or make them want to stop reading. If one part of a memorandum has to be exquisitely well written, it is the briefing. *Edit* and *rewrite* until the prose is a polished gem.

Another way writers can put their readers off right away is by the tone they adopt. An example would be taking a challenging or confrontational position with a reader who you know is hostile to your case. In such instances, it's better to work your case up more slowly.

10

Using Graphics

Designing Graphics

Charts, tables, and graphs are used to illustrate a comparison or contrast between a series of data or variables. A writer should choose to use them when, to repeat an old saw, "a picture will be worth a thousand words." The problem for most writers is that they often do not recognize when a tabular or graphic presentation would be much clearer and simpler than an explanation in prose. Here's an example of what I mean:

....

The results of the technical and economic evaluations are listed in the order of increasing annual cost in the attached summary sheets. Rego Computer and J&E Computers are lowest in cost. Rego Computer and Allied Electric are technically rated one and two, respectively. Allied Electric is about two times the cost of the two low vendors. An award based solely on the results of the invitation would recommend Rego Computer. However, a partial award to J&E Computers is also recommended to provide a back-up system, at negligible difference in cost, in the event Rego Computer is unable to meet our schedule requirements. In addition, it is recommended that Allied Electric be awarded an annual order for programs currently being run at Allied Electric facilities. The recommended authorization for Allied Electric provides funds to phase out Allied Electric usage over a 6-month period, which period is required to minimize loss of productivity and personnel retraining problems.

....

Now turn the page and look at a table the writer was able to come up with to organize these comparisons more simply.

Vendor	Cost	Technical Rating	Recommendations
Rego Computer	Lowest	First	_____ _____ _____ _____
J&E Computers	Same as Rego	Third or??	_____ _____ _____ _____
Allied Electric	Two times Rego & J&E Computers	Second	_____ _____ _____ _____

In this example, some prose would still be necessary to help the reader make sense of the table. The recommendations would be written in prose and perhaps a brief cover memorandum or summary paragraph would introduce the purpose of the table. Finally, the table should have a title that pinpoints its message.

In short, you should use a table, chart, or graph to explain relationships that do not easily lend themselves to prose explanation. Selecting what form of graphic to use, once you've identified the need for a visual presentation, will depend on your content.

Tables are used to organize information in a matrix or grid. The reader is usually invited to read both vertically and horizontally. Tables only imply relationships and are the least visual kind of graphic. They help your reader know how you've classified information.

Charts and graphs, on the other hand, *demonstrate* relationships visually. They should be used to reinforce messages that are not clear from tabular data alone.

Most charts are variations on the same forms: pie, bar, column, line, and dot. Each form illustrates certain kinds of relationships better than others.

Here's a matrix[1] that matches five standard types of comparisons (shown across the top) with the five basic chart forms (listed down the side).

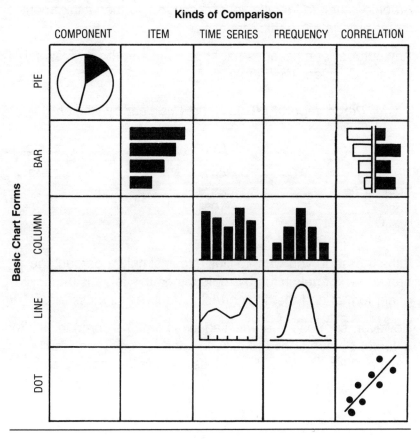

Figure 10.1.

[1]Gene Zelazny, *Say It with Charts: The Executive's Guide to Successful Presentations* (Homewood, Illinois: Dow Jones–Irwin, 1985), p. 27.

This matrix is an excellent illustration of the power of graphics. Think how many words it would take me to explain its content.

The problem report writers most often encounter when they decide to illustrate a point graphically is *identifying their message.* I've already noted that sometimes a futile attempt to explain a series of comparisons in prose may lead you to the realization that a graphic can make the point more simply and clearly. However, the most straightforward way to design a graphic is first to identify your message and then think about the appropriate graphic format.

Any number of messages might be illustrated by a given set of data. Consider this data:

Percentage of MBAs Hired This Year by Region

	Co. X	Co. Y
North	25%	35%
South	25%	30%
East	10%	20%
West	40%	15%

If the message you want to illustrate is simply a percentage breakdown of new hires by region, then this table is the appropriate format and the title correctly identifies its message.

However, suppose your message was that the companies hire different percentages of MBAs in each region. Then you'd need a different format to demonstrate this message clearly.

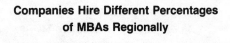

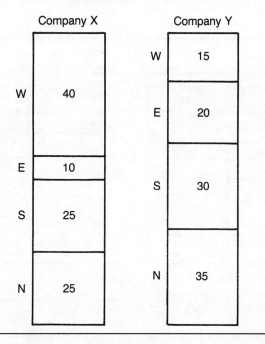

Figure 10.2.

Now suppose your message was that Company X hires its largest percentage of MBAs from the West, where Company Y hires its smallest percentage of MBAs.

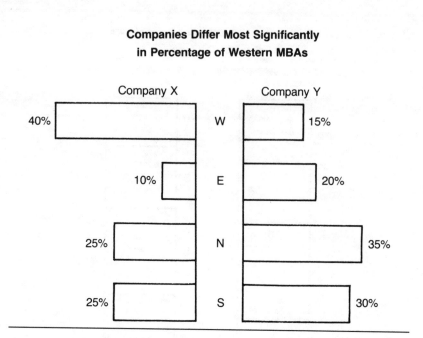

**Companies Differ Most Significantly
in Percentage of Western MBAs**

Figure 10.3.

The form your graphic will take depends entirely on your message. Without that message clearly in mind, you're flying blind. Or as one authority puts it: "Choosing a chart form without a message in mind is like trying to color coordinate your wardrobe while blindfolded."[2]

Sometimes report writers make problems for themselves needlessly with graphics. They know readers like them so they try to use them. In doing so, they sometimes miss the most fundamental point about graphics: readers like them *when they make a point clear*. Just like poorly written prose, a graphic without a clear message slows the reader down and impedes the report's readability.

---

[2]Zelazny, p. 11.

Helping the Reader Assimilate a Graphic

Once you've designed a graphic, you help your readers assimilate its message by:

- stating the message in a title
- placing the graphic where the reader needs to see it

In titling graphics, avoid general topic titles and instead pinpoint the message you want readers to see in the graphic. Good titles *instruct* the reader to look at something specific. Consider the same chart with different titles.

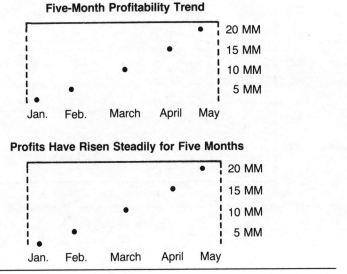

Figure 10.4.

The second chart will be easier for readers to comprehend because its title states its message more precisely. Chart titles must do more than state the topic: they must direct the readers' eyes to see something in the chart.

Since a general title will not direct readers' eyes, they may focus on a comparison you did not intend. For example:

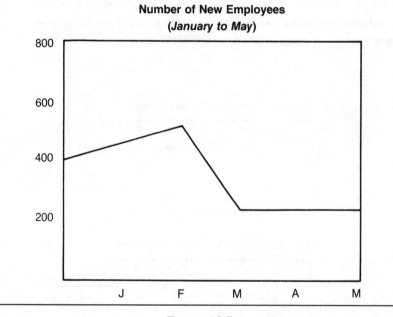

Number of New Employees
(January to May)

Figure 10.5.

Given such a general title, a reader might focus on one of several messages implied in the data:

- The number of new employees has decreased.
- The highest number of new employees was hired in February.

- The number of new employees dipped sharply in March.
- The same number of employees was hired in April and May.

You must tell readers which of these messages you consider important for them to see.

Once you pinpoint your message, the title itself states that message clearly and concisely, the way newspaper headlines do. Here are some topic titles that have been turned into instructive titles:

....

Topic title:	Percentage of Sales by Division
Instructive title:	Widget Division Accounts for 54% of Sales
Topic title:	Construction Demographic Trends
Instructive title:	New Construction Grows in the Southwest
Topic title:	Relationship of Owners' Salaries and Profits
Instructive title:	Owners' Salaries Are Weakening Company Profits

....

When writing titles, keep the tone factual. Avoid headlines that suggest the tabloid style: "New Construction Skyrockets in the Southwest."

Once you've designed your graphic and titled it, show it *at the exact moment* that you want readers to see it. In general, this means integrating the graphic into the report text.

The reason for this generalization is that a graphic loses some of its immediate illustrative power when readers must go searching for it. This applies to all sorts of graphics: pictures, diagrams, charts, flowcharts, graphs, or tables. Thus appendices are best used for supplemental information.

An exceptional situation might occur when you have many graphics to show and including them all in the text might fragment the report. In such cases, you would put the graphics in an appendix and cross-reference readers at the exact moment you want them to look at a particular graphic. In addition to titling each graphic in the appendix, you'd also label them in order: Appendix 1, Appendix 2, etc. Your cross-reference can refer to the shorter label rather than the longer title: "See Appendix I."

In longer research reports, the report is often printed and bound like a book. In such cases, graphics are usually given a page or part of a page next to the prose text in the same way that pictures and illustrations are displayed in a hardbound book. Readers are then cross-referenced to the page or place where they can find a particular graphic when they read the section of the text that explains its purpose.

Whether a graphic is integrated into the text or relegated to an appendix, *its point should be stated in the text* as well as in its title. This is most often accomplished by prefacing the graphic with a prose statement of its point, showing it, and then perhaps commenting further on its implications. Or you might provide a general introduction to the graphic in prose, show it, and then state its main point and comment on it.* You've seen me use both these approaches a number of times in this lesson. Let me recall one example to refresh your memory:

....

In titling graphics, avoid general topic titles and instead pinpoint the message you want readers to see in the graphic. Good titles instruct the reader to look at something specific. Consider the same chart with different titles.

---

*Sometimes when a graphic is integrated into the text, the title will be redundant and may be omitted.

Five-Month Profitability Trend

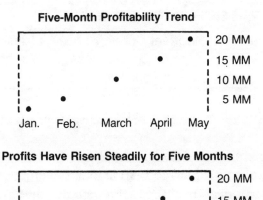

Profits Have Risen Steadily for Five Months

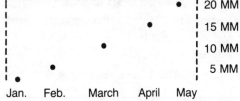

Figure 10.6.

The second chart will be easier for readers to comprehend because its title states its message more precisely. Chart titles must do more than state the topic: they must direct the reader's eyes to see something in the chart.

This time, I've italicized the point in the text that the graphic illustrates.

Always remember that stating a graphic's purpose clearly in the text and explaining its implications in readable prose remain your most powerful tools for helping readers assimilate it. Graphics should *never* be used as a substitute for stating a point and explaining it clearly in prose. The text is the most important part of the report and will always occupy the center stage.

Exercise, Part 1: Designing a Graphic Format

Perhaps the most important skill you'll need in designing graphics is the ability to recognize when a table, chart, or graph would help present your content better than prose alone. Then you need to be able to design an appropriate graphic format that conveys a message simply and, you hope, memorably.

Read the paragraph shown in the Example. I think you'll agree that one reason it's hard to read is that it attempts to explain a series of comparisons in prose. Present this message more simply and clearly. To do this, you'll need to:

- pinpoint the message you want to show in a graphic
- choose a form for the graphic
- state the message of the graphic in an instructive title
- combine the graphic with a prose commentary on its message

Example

The cost of the current JV Computer Training Tutorial is $50,000 a year. The Lark Tutorial is superior and we should consider installing it, even though initial installation would cost $60,000. The current JV Tutorial will continue to cost $50,000 each year, whereas the second year cost of the Lark Tutorial would be only $5,000 and $3,000 for each year thereafter. By installing the Lark Tutorial, we could save about $45,000 in the second year and about $47,000 for each year after that.

Your presentation: _____

_____

_____

_____

_____

_____

_____

_____

_____

_____

_____

Exercise, Part 2: Designing a Graphic Format

Three possible graphic revisions of the paragraph are shown below. Compare your revision with these. Then decide which one you think is the most effective, next effective, down to least effective. Be sure to include yours in the ranking; it may be better than any of these.

After you've judged all the examples, record your ranking in the spaces provided here. Also record the reasons for your decisions.

Your ranking:

Most effective _____	Why? _____	
Next effective _____	Why? _____	
Next effective _____	Why? _____	
Least effective _____	Why? _____	

Example 1

We should install the Lark Computer Training Tutorial because it's superior to ours and will be cheaper in the long run.

Comparative Costs

	This Year	*Next Year*	*Thereafter*
JV	*$50,000*	*$50,000*	*$50,000*
Lark	*$60,000*	*$ 5,000*	*$ 3,000*

Although we'll spend $10,000 more for Lark the first year, the ultimate savings after that will be enormous: $45,000 the second year and $47,000 per year for each subsequent year.

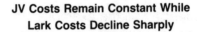

Example 2

I recommend installing the Lark Computer Training Tutorial in place of our JV Tutorial. As the accompanying graph shows, the initial cost of installation will be higher than the price we now pay for JV, but the savings in subsequent years will be substantial.

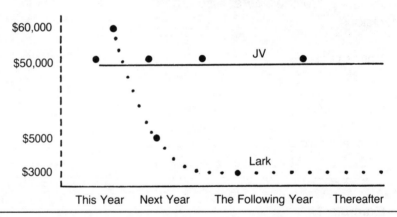

Figure 10.7.

Example 3

We should install the Lark Computer Training Tutorial in place of the JV Tutorial we now use. The columns in the chart below show that, after an initially higher cost of installation, Lark will be considerably cheaper in subsequent years than JV.

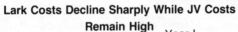

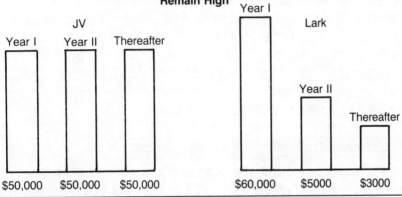

Figure 10.8.

Suggested Revisions: Designing a Graphic Format

Once again, I cannot provide commentary on your example, but I am providing commentary on the three examples shown. Use my comments to help you evaluate your example and your ranking of all the examples.

Example 1

This is probably the simplest and perhaps the clearest way to revise the example. The table clears up the major readability problem in the paragraph.

In addition to using a table to organize the cost comparisons, the writer introduces the table with a statement that directs the reader's attention to the salient point illustrated in the table—"cheaper in the long run." She also discusses some implications of the table afterwards. The table's general topic title, however, does not pinpoint its message and should be revised or omitted.

Example 2

The primary visual value of the line graph is the picture it presents of the decline in Lark's costs after one year. The instructive title reinforces this message. The prose introduction, however, centers on an aspect of the data that is not emphasized in the table: *savings*. The chart would be better introduced by a statement emphasizing the cost declines. The writer might then discuss the savings that result from these declines in a prose explanation following the chart.

Example 3

Some might argue that the data being presented are too simple for a graphic presentation of this sort. But you must admit that the columns illustrate the comparison more dramatically and perhaps more memorably than the other two charts. The prose introduction and the instructive title also dovetail nicely to direct the eye to the graphic's message.

When choosing a graphic presentation, you may find there are several that could work. You'll usually choose the one that's the simplest—in this case, the table is the simplest presentation. If, however, you're especially concerned about impact, you may choose "drama" as one of your criteria in designing a graphic.

Epilogue

Dear Reader:

Congratulations! You have now completed the equivalent of what you'd receive in most college-level or executive-level courses in business writing.

I had two major goals in writing this book. The first was to encourage you to write in your own voice rather than in a style that imitates someone else's voice. If you've learned nothing else from this book, I hope you've learned that it's okay to speak out and be yourself when you write.

I realize this is easier said than done. We've discussed why people fear being open and honest in their writing. And our great English literary tradition, which I've made reference to throughout this book, is both a burden and a gift. Most of us, when we write, feel the shadow of this tradition hanging over us. We think we will never write as well as John Milton, or Shakespeare, or perhaps even as well as our best friend who got an "A" in English. In short, we believe there's some sort of "absolute standard of good writing" floating out there in space, like a Platonic Idea, that we have little hope of measuring up to.

As I've mentioned before, though, what you should really do is develop your own standards and measure up to those. To do this, you should seek to learn from the accomplishments of other writers rather than merely imitating them. This is finally the only way you'll ever feel confident about your work or develop any real facility.

My second goal was, I think, more important. We live in an age when perhaps the most fundamental principle of good writing and, indeed, of all human communication has been forgotten. Communication happens when one human being connects, either positively or negatively, with another human being. Impersonal, gutless writing is the sign of a person in hiding. "Facilitating" the message, writing "the company way," "packaging" the message in a nonthreatening way—these and similar concepts of communication all add up to hiding, in my view. Or they imply manipulation, which is just an unethical form of hiding.

If you're going to write for the purpose of communicating, you'll have to come out into the open. And you'll need solid tools and techniques to start carving out your message.

I hope you've acquired some tools and gained some confidence. Enjoy!

Sincerely yours,

Olivia Stockard

Sources Cited

Burroughs, Edgar Rice. *Tarzan of the Apes*. New York: Ballantine Books, January 1976.

Ewing, David. *Writing for Results*. 2d edition. New York: John Wiley & Sons, 1979.

Fielden, John S. " 'What Do You Mean, You Don't Like My Style?' " *Harvard Business Review*, May–June 1982, pp. 128–138.

Greer, Germaine. *The Female Eunuch*. New York: McGraw-Hill, 1970.

Henze, Geraldine. *From Murk to Masterpiece: Style for Business Writing*. Homewood, Illinois: Richard D. Irwin, Inc., 1984.

How to Write Right for Us! United States Army Training and Doctrine Command. Fort Monroe, Virginia: August 1980.

Lanham, Richard A. *Revising Prose*. New York: Charles Scribner's Sons, 1979.

McCrum, Robert, Cran, William, and MacNeil, Robert. *The Story of English*. New York: Elisabeth Sifton Books, Viking, 1986.

Milton, John. "Areopagitica." Excerpted and reprinted in *The*

College Survey of English Literature, Shorter edition. Revised and ed. Alexander M. Witherspoon. New York: Harcourt, Brace & World, 1951.

Minto, Barbara. *The Pyramid Principle: Logic in Writing and Thinking*. United States of America: Minto International Inc., 1982.

Orwell, George. "Politics and the English Language." Reprinted in *A Collection of Essays by George Orwell*. New York: Harcourt, Brace, Jovanovich, Inc., Harbrace Paperbound Library, 1953.

Skyrms, Brian. *Choice and Chance: An Introduction to Inductive Logic.* Third Edition. Belmont, California: Wadsworth Publishing Company, 1986.

Sweetnam, Sherry. *The Executive Memo: A Guide to Persuasive Business Communications.* New York: John Wiley & Sons, 1986.

The New York Times. "Obituary of Dr. Rudolf Flesch," October 7, 1986.

The Price Waterhouse Guide to the New Tax Law. Introduction by Roscoe L. Egger, Jr. New York: Bantam Books, 1986.

Zelazny, Gene. *Say It with Charts: The Executive's Guide to Successful Presentations*. Homewood, Illinois: Dow Jones–Irwin, 1985.

Index

Index

Index

Index